THE SUCCESSFUL TEACHER

The Successful Teacher

Essays in Secondary School Instruction

JAMES L. KELLY

EDITOR

The Iowa State University Press

AMES

Printed by The Iowa State University Press, Ames, Iowa 50010

First edition, 1982

Library of Congress Cataloging in Publication Data
Main entry under title

The Successful teacher.

    Includes bibliographies and index.
    1. High school teaching—Addresses, essays, lectures. I. Kelly, James L., 1942–
LB1625.S85   373.11′02   81–23651
ISBN 0-8138-0196-6   AACR2

C O N T E N T S

CONTRIBUTORS

James E. Albrecht
Principal, Northern University High School
Professor, College of Education
University of Northern Iowa
Cedar Falls, Iowa 50613

Leander Brown
Assistant Professor, Educational Psychology
  and Foundations
University of Northern Iowa
Cedar Falls, Iowa 50613

Timothy M. Cooney
Assistant Professor, Teaching,
  Northern University High School
University of Northern Iowa
Cedar Falls, Iowa 50613

James L. Kelly
Assistant Professor, Teaching,
  Northern University High School
University of Northern Iowa
Cedar Falls, Iowa 50613

Alvah M. Kilgore
Associate Professor, Secondary Education
University of Nebraska-Lincoln
Lincoln, Nebraska 68588

Charles Moore
Dean of Students, Anoka-Hennepin
  Independent School District
Anoka, Minnesota 55303

Toni E. Santmire
Associate Professor, Educational Psychology
  and Measurements
University of Nebraska-Lincoln
Lincoln, Nebraska 68588

Richard F. Strub
Associate Professor, Teaching,
  Northern University High School
University of Northern Iowa
Cedar Falls, Iowa 50613

L. James Walter
Associate Professor, Secondary Education
University of Nebraska-Lincoln
Lincoln, Nebraska 68588

P R E F A C E

The idea for this book was conceived while I was working with student teachers at the University of Nebraska-Lincoln. The questions the beginning teachers were asking and the discussions that ensued seemed to be the same questions and discussions I had had many years before with my student teachers. It became obvious that while times had changed and education had changed the common concerns of beginning teachers continued to remain the same.

This experience prompted me more than any one thing to ask authors who are successful teachers in their own right to write chapters that would help to answer the questions of beginning teachers. While the manuscript was designed initially to fit the needs of beginning teachers, it should be noted that experienced teachers have many of the same concerns and, therefore, we, the authors, hope this assemblage of essays can be used effectively by all teachers.

James L. Kelly

INTRODUCTION

What does it take to be a successful teacher? Because success tends to lead toward continued success, it is important for teachers to begin well and then to perpetuate their successful beginnings.

The Successful Teacher: Essays in Secondary School Instruction deals with educational issues that seem to recycle continuously. Each chapter is directed toward a specific issue, one frequently brought up by both beginning and experienced teachers.

Chapter 1 identifies the way in which adolescents develop intellectually by Piagetian stages. While intellectual development is gradual, the developmental stages are evident and teachers must be able to recognize the signs and proceed with the learner accordingly.

Chapter 2 discusses values education and gives excellent, related examples. Values education surfaces in the classroom many times. If properly handled, the outcomes enhance student learning and help with effective teaching. Chapter 2 is an excellent follow-up to Chapter 1 in that it discusses Kohlberg's model of moral development, which, like intellectual development, is a sequential process, both tending to develop together.

Chapter 2 also identifies the five values education approaches: inculcation, moral development, clarification, action learning, and analysis.

Chapter 3 relates to characteristics of humanistic education. Knowing how students develop intellectually and morally are precepts for humanistic education. Humanistic education focuses on helping students recognize their own potential. Effective teachers who relate to humanistic instruction are able to create an environment where learning is a pleasurable experience for both students and teachers.

Chapter 4 helps teachers to prepare to work with a multicultural society. It is important for teachers to be aware of the dimensions of working with diverse groups within our society. Since there is virtually no formal training for working with various ethnic groups in teacher preparation programs, Chapter 4 is a valuable reference for teachers who may work with such students.

Chapter 5, written by an administrator with twenty-six years of experience, synthesizes the things successful teachers do. The simple task of making assignments is carefully rendered for each teacher to see. Classroom management, large- and small-group discussions, and classroom environments are presented. Each section provides the reader with concise ways and means for effective and successful teaching.

Teachers are continually required to make decisions. Chapter 6 relates to the types of decisions teachers and prospective teachers need to make on a daily basis. Forms for evaluating instructional effectiveness also are presented.

Chapter 7 explains how teachers plan, use, and evaluate a teaching strategy. If the procedure-by-procedure approach of this chapter is applied, teachers should be able to establish a teaching strategy for any given unit of study. Various teaching model families are presented, showing their direct and indirect application. These models are based on theories about how students learn. The theories relate back to Chapter 1.

Chapters 7 and 6 are closely related also: sound decision making is required for establishing correct teaching strategy.

The final chapter, Chapter 8, presents a scheme for classroom management. Questions of discipline are foremost among the problems presented to student teacher advisers. The problem is of real concern to beginning teachers, to all teachers. Undoubtedly, discipline is effective only when a clear-cut management scheme is adopted. Chapter 8 establishes the procedures needed for creating such a program.

The Successful Teacher: Essays in Secondary School Instruction covers eight basic topics related to education. Today, school systems and teachers alike are being held more accountable for their instructional prowess. As teachers read through the pages of this book, it is hoped they will find information that will help them to become more successful and more effective teachers and educators.

James L. Kelly

THE SUCCESSFUL TEACHER

1

INTELLECTUAL DEVELOPMENT
OF THE ADOLESCENT

Toni E. Santmire

Teachers often comment on the sense of accomplishment they receive from being able to help a student develop into a serious and logical thinker with mature ideas and interests in a subject matter area. However, such development is, at the same time, the source of many of the problems associated with teaching adolescents. Moreover, such development does not occur overnight. There is some apparent backward as well as forward progress, and the process is often confusing, irritating, and even painful for all concerned. Nonetheless, one of the most exciting things about teaching adolescents is the intellectual growth that usually occurs during this period.

In my experience with teachers I have found that the descriptions of mature formal operational thinking and the concrete operations that precede it are not written in terms useful for classroom application. Usually these stages are discussed in terms of performance on scientific or mathematical problems, problems difficult to relate to performance in other subject matter and seemingly unrelated to other typical classroom behaviors. The fact is that the change from concrete to formal thinking can take place in any subject matter area and in any interpersonal area, and the change is expressed in ways that are identifiable in typical classroom events.

Understanding how classroom behavior relates to intellectual development can help teachers plan instructional activities that will be effective in promoting both current learning and later intellectual growth.

Changes in adolescent thinking occur in a regular sequence. Each of the steps is marked by a change in the way the information is organized by the individual and each grows out of the thought processes that preceded it. Each change makes possible new intellectual abilities but also places limits on what students can understand. These limitations are as important for teaching as the abilities.

HOW STUDENTS ORGANIZE INFORMATION

The sequence of development observed in adolescents can be divided into four steps or stages. In Piagetian terms these stages are called <u>Unconsolidated Concrete Operations</u>, <u>Consolidated Concrete Operations</u>, <u>Early Formal Operations</u>, and <u>Late Formal Operations</u>. They usually begin sometime after age eleven and they are rarely completed prior to the early twenties.

Unconsolidated concrete operations are characteristic primarily of preadolescents. This stage needs to be examined in a discussion of adolescent intellectual development because some 12- and 13-year-old students show this type of thinking in the early junior high school years.

Late formal operations are characteristic of individuals who have begun to use their knowledge as adults in a professional way and so it is not normally attained until after high school. Some juniors and seniors in high school show beginning characteristics of this stage, and teachers need to know how to recognize and encourage this development.

Although development is discussed here in terms of stages it is important to keep in mind that the process is not as incisive as these divisions might imply. In the first place development is gradual. Second, development is uneven in many individuals, and a person using formal operations in one area may still be quite concrete in another. Sometimes the stress associated with change gives rise to what may appear to be regression to earlier stages.

Unconsolidated Concrete Operations

The thought of the student in the unconsolidated concrete operations stage is best characterized by its organization into categories or sequences based upon the individual's own experience. Each category or sequence is a system or organization within itself, unrelated in the mind of the individual with other systems of organization used at other times. Thus, the person can think in terms of only one such system at a time.

For example, one sequential system is that of the relationships among generations of families--from grandparents, to parents, to children, etc. This is extended to aunts, uncles, and cousins. Another category system, which individuals may learn during this period, is the system by which one organizes the animal kingdom. Students learn, for example, about mammals, birds, insects, and amphibia as categories. Further subcategories of those are then learned. The animal kingdom may be organized also by the normal food consumed: carnivores, herbivores, and omnivores; this animal category system is different from that of mammals, and the unconsolidated concrete individual has a difficult time keeping both in mind at once. The systems are basically independent of each other in that person's thought.

Because these categories originate from individual experience, they are given the status of being factual and real. This causes individuals in this stage to think that thoughts in their minds are real. They sometimes have a hard time distinguishing fantasy from fact. Each category system may also be used as a whole at any time. Thus, the general is given the same status as the specific. This means, for example, that concrete examples are often given in place of definitions. When asked to define a mammal an individual in this stage may say, "Well, it's like a dog or a cat."

The tendency for students at this stage to organize information into unrelated categories or compartments results in some typical classroom characteristics. In terms of learning content, these students focus only on one instructional objective at a time. For example, they see learning to spell as one activity and learning new word meanings as another. This means that knowledge does not necessarily transfer from one activity to the other. These students are at their best when learning facts and how to categorize or sequence them with other facts. Since there is always more than one category system that can be used to organize given facts, these students respond best when the way of organizing is defined by the instructor. Because they believe their orientation to these categories is descriptive of the real world,

these students believe there is always a right answer;
answers are either right or wrong; and the adult knows
what is right. They become confused, negative, and
disoriented by ambiguity.

The compartmentalization of category systems also
has implications for classroom management. Students often
do not see the relationship of activities to each other
in a sequence and so need to have instructions repeated
for each new activity. They continually have to ask the
teacher what to do next, sometimes even when the
instructions are written out. They find transitions
disorganizing and can become disorderly at such times.
Only after a sequence of activities has been repeated
several times do they remember the sequence.

When students at this stage are confused as to what
they should be doing, or when an activity is too difficult
for them, they will be at a loss. Sometimes they will
just sit. At other times they become negatively dependent
and "whiney," asking for adult attention. At still other
times, they will be captured by peer activities,
unconsciously getting drawn into the activity. They
cannot remember adult instructions for long, particularly
when the activity they are supposed to be doing is too
difficult for them or when there is no defined activity,
such as when they have to just sit and wait. Thus, they
conform to such adult instructions as, "Go to your seat
and wait until I get to you." But they get right out
of their seat when something distracts them if the teacher
has taken too long to get there. It is not that they
are being deliberately disobedient; they just move into
another situational system depending upon what they see.

As these students learn new category systems and
ways of doing things they begin to have more and more
ways of organizing information available to them. They
have more ways to respond to classroom situations. This
means that as soon as the teacher gives instructions they
can figure out what is expected of them and respond in
ways they have learned previously. On their own they
can obtain support or figure out what is expected.
Students who have acquired these stable and broad
categories through repetition and consistency in the
environment during the period in which they were
unconsolidated concrete operational now move to the
threshold of adolescence: consolidated concrete
operations.

Consolidated Concrete Operations

The thought of individuals who are in a consolidated concrete operational stage is in many respects like their thought in the unconsolidated stage. It is still compartmentalized. That is, the category systems they use are still unrelated to each other and they still have the tendency to confuse the general and specific. They are still fact-oriented and reality-oriented. Information is still sorted into what the child sees as the right categories or sequences of actions and once organized it is hard to reorganize. But, because of the greater breadth of the categories and their greater number, the situations they encounter that are not organizable in some way are fewer. This makes the students much less dependent and much more self-confident.

Because these students are still right-, wrong-, and fact-oriented, they like content that is primarily organized around descriptions of reality. Given the appropriate category system, they can now find examples on their own without being distracted by irrelevancies. They can search for information in reading if told what information is relevant, and they can begin to paraphrase material instead of simply copying it. They can also, if assisted, build up new categories or ways of seeing things. Their discussions consist mostly of giving examples of things rather than in making generalizations. They do not like to discuss issues or theories since these imply no right answer. Their writing consists mostly of descriptions of events.

In terms of classroom management these students are, in many ways, a joy to work with. They need enough teacher direction to get started—to know what sequence of activities is being carried out and how they fit together. Then the students can go off on their own and work independently. They may be at the teacher's elbow after each step to check that they have done it right, but then, reassured, they go back to work. Activities that are self-paced and self-contained are liked. Completing units of work gives them a sense of accomplishment and they often compare notes with their peers on how many packets were completed. However, because finishing an assignment is important, they have difficulty if they are interrupted before finishing it. They don't want to stop and they have trouble getting started again.

Ambiguous situations make these students feel very uncomfortable. They want clearly stated rules for classroom behavior and get quite upset at what they view as uneven enforcement of rules by the teacher. For most students at this stage, being different is unthinkable, whether from adults or peers. Consequently, when classroom situations are ambiguous and they are not getting enough direction from teachers, these students become peer distracted and unmanageable. They cannot handle more than one or two peers at a time without getting overstimulated unless all are doing the same thing.

Learning and consolidating broad category systems to organize information is the very condition that leads to the development of adolescent thought. As the students learn more ways of organizing the same information, eventually they realize there might be more than one way to categorize a given set of facts. For example, an animal can be categorized as either a herbivore or a mammal. The problem is that the concrete operational system has no way of deciding the correct category to use. Of course the adult knows that this is decided by the nature of the problem being dealt with but the early adolescent does not know this. It is the necessity of finding out which system is right that leads to the development of early formal operations.

Early Formal Operations

In early formal operational students, thought processes are organized in terms of the various alternative ways in which information or situations might simultaneously be seen. That is, when faced with a given animal, the student no longer knows quite what to do with it. Earlier, in consolidated concrete operations, the students would simply have put it into the category they happened to be using at the moment, or the one the teacher told them to use, or the one they were most familiar with. Now students can see that there is more than one category system they might use but they don't know which is appropriate. There is thus a reduction in the certainty with which students approach situations and an increase in dependency. At first students look to the teacher to define which is right, but still, they think about the other alternatives. The doubt raises questions in the students' minds as to why the teacher chose the alternative he or she did. Now begins an argumentative phase in which the students construct alternatives merely for the sake of generating alternatives.

No longer are students content to learn only what they are told as facts. They begin to see alternative ways of looking at things. At first when students realize these alternatives they think they must be poor students because they don't know the answers. This leads to a decrease in self-esteem and a need to ask teachers to define what is right. However, this tends to backfire on teachers because no matter what they come up with, students still seem to be able to think of alternatives. Because students are thinking in terms of concrete facts, they are unable to understand why teachers choose the alternatives they choose--they can see only that there is an alternative. In a way this means that the adult can never satisfy the arguments of adolescents in this stage. The adolescents realize that the adults do not have all of the answers and that they can think of alternatives to everything that the adult comes up with. Now the adolescents feel they have acquired adult status. Their questioning becomes increasingly generalized until they will not accept anything.

In terms of content, adolescents in early formal operations want to be able to do two things: (1) explore alternative ways of viewing the same situation, and (2) express and defend their own alternatives. They no longer want _facts_ to be learned; they want the _whys_ to be discussed. For example, why in one situation do we categorize a given animal as a mammal and why in another do we use the carnivore classification? They want to compare their own thought with that of both adults and peers. Group discussion techniques, comparisons among groups or individuals, and essays begin to be effective teaching techniques.

This period is one of self-definition for adolescents. They use the expression of their ideas as a means of defining possible ways of thinking about things. Because they can and do generate alternatives, they can become quite argumentative, questioning, and even disrespectful of authority. They also become quite peer oriented, questioning their loyalty to each other and exploring differences in the ways others think. This can lead to problems in classroom management. Adolescents not given the opportunity for self-expression may become negative and hostile, rebelling against learning

anything. The most positive students in this stage tend
to simply memorize or learn by rote and become
disinterested students, channeling their energies into
areas where the opportunities for self-expression are
greater--usually social activities. Peers now become
a real interference in classroom affairs. Students want
to talk with their peers more than they want to do the
work required.

But, although students in this stage tend to <u>want</u>
to do things their own way, they do not yet know <u>what</u>
their own way is. This stage is more defined by
opposition to what is traditional or expected than by
the positive generation of specific alternatives.
Consequently, when teachers give the students freedom
to set up their own projects or study plans, nothing comes
of it. I so often have heard teachers say in
exasperation, "When students come up and ask if they have
to do what has been assigned, and I say it is all right
for them to suggest something else, they never propose
anything!" This paradoxical behavior is a function of
the weakness of the thought organization of this stage.
Students are not yet able to define the problem and thus
to determine which alternative organizational system is
appropriate to use.

Students at this stage need to learn two things.
First, they need to know that all the alternatives they
generate are, in fact, alternative ways of organizing
the information. If they do not realize this, they will
permanently lose confidence in their own knowledge.
Consequently, their generation of alternatives, with its
sometimes unpleasant behavioral accompaniments, must be
tolerated and even supported. It does mean that they
will argue with us, that we will be exasperated with them
for not listening to reason at times, and that sometimes
it will seem there is arguing ad infinitum.

Second, adolescents come to recognize the arguments
that make sense and answer the questions they have about
which category systems should be used in given situations
to solve given problems. They need to learn how to argue
logically, how to analyze problems and arrive at relevant
solutions, and how to take alternative solutions into
account. These are the skills leading to the next stage.
It is the process of questioning, proposing solutions,
and finding out which solutions do or do not work that
leads to an understanding of how the problem solving

process works. In this stage, adolescents often have
to make their own mistakes and find out for themselves.
They need the freedom and support to do so.

Late Formal Operations
The consideration of alternative category systems
that might be used to analyze a given situation in the
early formal operations stage leads the adolescents at
this stage to consider these different category systems
and how they interrelate with each other. This now allows
them to identify the problem a given situation presents;
determine the relevant categories that might apply;
hypothesize how they interrelate; and devise empirical
tests to determine which is the case; in short, to be
truly experimental in approach. Thus logic becomes fully
developed. Now, when individuals are presented with
information, they no longer make a prejudgment about what
category it might belong to. Instead they look at what
use is to be made of the information and they analyze
it into categories relevant to that use. The individual
no longer approaches learning in terms of learning facts,
but in terms of answers to problems and how they hold
up under different conditions.
    Students at this stage are beyond questioning for
the sake of questioning. They look at how new information
relates to what they already know; they determine whether
it fits their existing hypotheses about what is operating
in a given situation; and they modify their thought or
actions accordingly. In these students search for new
knowledge is purposeful and directed. It is based on
whether they can fit new facts into existing frameworks.
These students begin to fit subjects together into bodies
of knowledge and to think like mature adults. This means
they learn what they want to learn, think for themselves,
and begin to make up their own minds about what they think
about a given subject matter. They are becoming
selective, deciding for themselves what it is they think
is important.

THE CLASSROOM ENVIRONMENT AND THE PROMOTING OF GROWTH
    The described sequence of intellectual development
and characteristic behaviors usually begins, as we have
noted, sometime after age eleven and is rarely completed
prior to the early twenties.

Research shows that some adults have not yet completed the final, <u>sophisticated</u> learning stage and that education significantly contributes to attaining full intellectual development. Research points to the fact that the sequence of stages does not progress automatically; that the environment plays a significant role in development.

If we look at how change occurs from stage to stage, another fact begins to emerge. We see that not only is the environment important in promoting development, but also that the characteristics of the environment that promote growth differ from stage to stage. The implications of this are far-reaching. It means that when students are at different stages they will require different things to make further growth possible. It means that the same teaching techniques, classroom activities, and materials will not be equally effective for all students either in promoting learning or in facilitating further development.

At any stage of development there are stage-specific ways of organizing experience; this means things will be understood in particular ways. Therefore students need an environment organized so they can understand it. At the same time, they need specific environments to help them progress to the next stage. Students need environments matched to their stage of development, both in terms of current characteristics and future growth.

Based on the descriptions of the organization of thought and how growth occurs, we will describe what a classroom environment matched to that stage would be like and how it would promote growth. The differences are quite striking.

Unconsolidated Concrete Operations

At this stage students are learning adult category systems. They fit information into the category systems they already know and do not see relationships with other possible category systems. To grow they need to learn many such reliable systems and then to use them in organizing new content.

A classroom matched to students at this stage, first of all establishes clearly what the learning activity is. Students are not asked to learn more than one thing at a time, or to remember more than one step in a sequence of activities. Routines that are repeated daily (with variations, once established) help these students gain self-control. Because these students tend to get caught up in whatever they see, they work best in classrooms where everyone is doing the same thing--or where differences are clearly set out and "the right thing to do."

Students at this stage are using three basic thinking activities: classification, seriation, and one-to-one correspondence. Secure learning of content will occur when learning activities make use of these skills one at a time. For example, geography content about a given country could include such activities as making lists of geographical features (lakes, cities, states, and rivers) (classification); plotting a trip across the country (seriation); or copying the names of geographical features onto a blank map (one-to-one correspondence). Correct spelling of the important names could be reinforced by unscrambling the words to match a correctly spelled list at the bottom of the page. Word searches and crossword puzzles can also be used to reinforce content and spelling.

Students at this stage have no sense of what the more general or important parts of a lesson are. They need someone to select the important things or they will learn only what strikes them. Consequently, when reading for facts or watching a film, they need study guides. These need to be keyed directly to the content by such cues as page numbers, key concepts or words, and copy work.

It is also important for teachers to realize that these students base their understanding on their own experience. Consequently they will learn best if the categories used are connected with that experience. Teachers need to listen to their students to see what spontaneous category systems are used and help them reorganize these to be consistent with adult usage.

Attention also needs to be paid to articulating content. The same content needs to be organized several different ways so that alternatives are experienced. For example, as described before, the category systems using herbivores and mammals could each be used when grouping animals. Eventually, in consolidated concrete operations, these two systems will no longer be seen as mutually exclusive.

Such an environment will help students build up the categories and extended routines they require in order to make the transition to the next stage. This growth

is facilitated by the teacher's encouraging students to
follow the routines on their own whenever they can. That
is, as the students learn the categories that are used
and the classroom routines, the teacher can and should
relax direction-giving and teacher imposed structure.
When something different is being done, directions need
to be action oriented. If the new activities can make
use of components of old ones, this also increases student
familiarity and promotes growth and flexibility.

Consolidated Concrete Operations

Students in this stage have had sufficient organized
experience to understand a large variety of classroom
routines and activities. This enables them to follow
new routines on their own once they have been explained.
They organize each set of activities as one large sequence
and can follow the directions on their own so long as
they can handle the content involved. These same
principles are true for content. By this time the
students have sufficient knowledge of the various content
areas to know the major category systems used in any given
subject area. Thus they know what major categories to
use when organizing new content. For example, they know
such things as numbers and how to manipulate them; basic
political and physical geographic categories; major
categories of scientific investigation; and major
children's literature selections.

It is this knowledge that makes students of this
stage generally compliant. However, they still rely on
external organization and do become discipline problems
when it is not there. Therefore they need classrooms
that have clearly established rule structures and
behavioral expectations. But, it should be emphasized,
they do now have a broader base of content and behavioral
systems to operate from.

They need to have classroom organization and learning
activities clearly set forth in terms of what is to be
done and the content categories and/or sequences clearly
specified. For example, these students can do a character
analysis in a novel by looking at descriptions of that
character in various places and combining the impressions
they create into a composite description. Students can
read material on a new country or geographic area and
search for information about important geographic/
political/historical features. Their knowledge of numbers
and the basic operations on numbers is well enough
established that they can begin looking at the

interrelations among the operations (that is, addition
and substraction are reciprocal; fractions can be added
or subtracted). Thus, they learn new things by applying
to new situations knowledge already possessed.

Growth from this stage to the next occurs as students
come to recognize that more than one classroom routine
or activity could serve to attain some goal. Similarly,
with content, students come to realize that there is more
than one way of categorizing events. This again is
promoted by clearly organized instructional environments
matched as described above. As students become confident
within these environments, they become increasingly sure
of themselves and they are then able to proceed on their
own.

They will begin, all on their own, to come up with
alternatives. This marks the transition to the next
stage. Again the response of the teacher is critical.
If the teacher responds by reasserting the already
existing structure the student can become very comfortable
at this stage. To promote further development the teacher
needs to recognize the students' alternatives as valid
and to allow some exploration. Of course this exploration
needs to be within the limits of reasonable behavior and
the subject matter, but it needs to occur.

Early Formal Operations

This stage is probably the most difficult and, at
the same time, the most exciting for both teachers and
students. Students at the beginning of this stage are
insecure and have low self-esteem due to their ability
to see alternatives and yet the inability to see
resolutions. They feel they should know the solution
and that this inability is their fault. This causes them
to be defensive (and thus somewhat loud and offensive)
when they do present alternatives, yet at the same time
they are dependent and need help or "attention" to resolve
their questions.

They question or find alternatives to both classroom
rules and content. The central task of this stage is
the development of problem solving processes that will
allow the individual to find ways to choose among
alternatives. Consequently, students need environments
that freely permit a consideration of alternatives and
provide help in the definition and solving of problems.

A central limitation on thought at this stage also
needs to be considered. Students at this stage need to
have goals and means set forth before alternatives can

be seen. That is, they cannot generate alternatives
unless they know to what they are providing an
alternative.

With these considerations in mind, a matched
classroom environment for early formal operational
students is one in which the teacher has clearly thought
through content objectives and has designed classroom
materials, activities, and organizational routines to
meet these objectives. The teacher must then be open
to alternatives and questions as they arise from
students. Since students are often overly defensive and
insecure, leading to either overassertion or excessive
timidity or dependency, the teacher must be very accepting
and supportive of students during this stage.

Students grow through exploration of their own and
others' alternatives. Consequently student self-
expression needs to be encouraged and, because they are
insecure, never ridiculed but accepted and supported.
Opportunities for sharing students' ideas with peers and
others need to be made available.

In terms of subject matter, students at this stage
can profit from activities that compare and contrast
various categories or points of view. For example,
similarities and differences in creation myths or in
adolescent problems in other cultures, times, and places
could be studied. Different cultural solutions to
geographical or political problems or pros and cons of
issues in history all provide useful content, particularly
if students are asked to generate and defend their own
position. This is the ideal time in mathematics for the
introduction of algebra, dealing as it does with the
general properties of the number system. Solutions for
unknowns become an extension of the interrelations of
algorithms learned earlier and then the general properties
can be used to understand why solutions work. In science
curricula this becomes an ideal stage for the introduction
of explanatory systems for observations. This is
especially true for those that are difficult to grasp,
such as speeds of falling bodies, repulsion of charged
particles, or mechanical advantages in levers and pulleys.
Where students have not been exposed to the concepts
before, the observations must precede the explanations
so as to generate the "why" questions.

The alternatives of this level are not alternative
theories, but rather alternative sequences, categories,
or correspondences in events. The problems students have
to learn to solve are the ways to decide which category

is appropriate or how two systems operate together. For example, realizing that when the topic under investigation is organization of the nervous system or evolution, the major subdivisions of the animal kingdom (mammals, insects) is most useful. When the topic is ecology or place in the food chain, it may be more relevant to consider food preferences as a major classification scheme. Thus the nature of the question being dealt with determines that which is relevant.

Similarly, when the goal of instruction is a comparison of different points of view on slavery to be obtained by summarizing newspaper articles, a student might want to do some alternative activity. A workable alternative might be to compare two speeches in which contrasting viewpoints were presented.

It is important for teachers to be open to alternatives, flexible, and emotionally positive and supportive. It is also important for teachers to know what their goals are, to be clear about these goals and consistent in maintaining them. Many alternatives generated by students at this stage are inappropriate because of a lack of knowledge and a lack of problem-solving skills. When teachers help students articulate their alternatives and, when necessary, explore them, they help students see when they are appropriate and when not. At the same time, when students generate alternatives, they need to have a secure standard against which they can test the validity of their ideas. It is this that teachers provide when they do not let students "get away with" something inappropriate.

Thus, during this stage of development, teachers need to be open to student ideas and to assist them in exploring alternatives within the context of a firm set of goals against which all alternatives are evaluated. Students enter the next stage by generating, articulating, and evaluating alternatives. Now they no longer need to question merely for the sake of questioning, to generate alternatives simply to show that alternatives can be generated. Instead they begin to focus on the purpose or goal of the activity and to evaluate alternatives in terms of reaching a goal.

Late Formal Operations

Once students realize reasons exist for selecting various category systems, they begin to search for those reasons. They want to identify the problem and solve it rather than just identify potential categories. Thus

they become more interested in the questions or problems
than the facts. Their study becomes more directed and
purposeful. They become interested in theories as answers
to the questions and in developing means for testing
theories. Thus late high school students read literature
more for understanding how others have dealt with the
issues of life rather than reading for the specific
action. Then they begin to understand how plot,
characterization, and action can by used to deal with
those issues. In the social sciences, they begin to see
different political systems as different theories about
the nature of human beings and their societies. In
science, they examine alternative theories for various
phenomena and subject them to empirical tests. In
mathematics, they look at the development of the ideas
of establishing proofs in geometry and more advanced
mathematics.

As such developments take place, teaching needs to
focus on these major themes, issues, or theories.
Students at this stage become very impatient with "fact-
level" teaching. Facts are seen primarily as support
for points of view rather than as something to be learned
for themselves. So long as students of this stage can
pursue their interests in subject matter, discipline
problems become almost nonexistent. These students are
also less sensitive to teaching methods. They do not
mind lectures because they can deal with issues just as
well in that format as in reading, and sometimes even
better than in discussion. Discussions are useful when
all members of the group are interested in the content,
but these students do not want to discuss just to be
discussing. In addition, labs for the sake of repeating
someone else's observations are generally not useful,
but labs for the purpose of testing theoretical hypotheses
are.

Adolescents who fall into this group exhibit
characteristics more common to college students than to
high school students. Attainment of this level of
intellectual development is, in some sense, what
adolescent maturation is all about.

A FINAL WORD
In actual classroom environments, the situation will
be more complex than it might seem from the discussion
here. In the first place, the age of onset and rate of
progression through the various stages is highly

individual. Some students begin the adolescent transition as early as fifth grade, others not until ninth. Some are basically formal operational by ninth grade, others never attain fully equilibrated logical abilities.

A second complicating factor is that, even within a given individual, development may be uneven. For example, some individuals move toward formal operations in mathematical and/or scientific subjects, but remain quite concrete in social relationships. Others do just the opposite. In fact, data seem to indicate that mixed stages across various subject matter areas are quite common within individuals.

In addition, the stress associated with change sometimes causes individuals to temporarily regress, that is, to behave in ways more immature than usual. This means that students who are normally being somewhat formal operational may sometimes appear quite concrete operational.

The variations, both within and across individuals, mean that secondary teachers are faced with a wide variety of stages in adolescent behavior in any given classroom and this complicates the teaching job. Teachers need to be able to identify from day to day and situation to situation where students are in the adolescent transition. The purpose of the tracing of the stages has been partly to provide teachers with the behavioral descriptions that would permit them to identify everyday classroom behavior more easily.

Adapting instruction and classroom environments to the needs of adolescents is beneficial to their development. It is certainly not easy, but the rewards are great.

REFERENCES AND SUGGESTED READINGS
Elkind, D. Children and Adolescents: Interpretive Essays on Jean Piaget. 2d ed. New York: Oxford University Press, 1974.
Hunt, D. E. "A conceptual systems change model and its application to education." In O. J. Harvey, ed. Experience, Structure, and Adaptability. New York: Springer, 1966.
Hunt, D. E., and Sullivan, E. V. Between Psychology and Education. Hinsdale, Ill.: Dryden, 1974.
Inhelder, B., and Piaget, J. The Growth of Logical Thinking from Childhood to Adolescence. New York: Basic Books, 1958.

2

VALUES AND THE ADOLESCENT

Timothy M. Cooney

Students' lives are filled today with a large variety of experiences from which they sort out what they like and dislike, and by which they develop either positive or negative attitudes toward certain experiences. Eventually, these attitudes develop into general guides to their behavior.

Today's students have a more difficult time than ever before in selecting what is truly of value. As members of an affluent society, they are offered an inexhaustible selection of consumer goods and services. Trying to make a decision about these goods and services is difficult even for adults. For example, a person walking into a supermarket has to decide not only what products to buy, but also which brand to select. In many cases this decision is made more difficult by comparisons between the regular size and the economy size, or between volume, or mass, and price.

Attempting to decide what is good and bad societal behavior is equally difficult. Almost daily our students view and hear by the mass media that the world is full of social disorder and unrest. They are told not to break the laws of society, yet they hear that some governmental officials and corporations have not followed these rules. Many movies and books display various aspects of deviant behavior in our society--murder, rape, and stealing. It is little wonder that young people today find themselves in strong conflict when trying to resolve what they should and should not value.

Two major aspects contributing to the development of our students' values are the family and the school. (Many other experiences also influence students' value

21

development: peer groups, religious education, etc.,
but to list them all here is, of course, not possible.)
The family was and still is the most important influence
on a person's value system. However, the structure of
the family has changed drastically in the last few
decades. This is exemplified by the high rates of
divorce, separation, and one-parent families. Family
members tend to share less time together and spend more
time doing their own thing. Therefore, the family
influence on each individual's values has decreased in
most cases.

Schools have established rules that tell students
what the administration considers to be proper behavior.
Moreover, teachers have their own values and attitudes
which are reflected by their opinions and behavior. These
definitely will influence students' thoughts and actions.
In other words, schools are not and cannot be value free.

Therefore, if educators influence the value choices
of students intentionally and unintentionally through
teachers' and administrators' rules, words, and actions,
I believe it is essential that time be allotted for
students to examine their own beliefs. Value development
is a very personal process that is filled with much
conflict and frustration. It requires time for a person
to think through values decisions alone or within the
context of group interaction.

Schools generally tend to concentrate on teaching
facts and concepts and, in many cases, try to stay clear
of the affective domain. In the cases where schools have
paid some attention to certain values and attitudes, it
has been by a process of inculcation. This approach will
do nothing to promote value decision making. Values
decisions must be made freely by considering various
alternatives before a final selection is formulated.
Therefore, I recommend to you an educational methodology
that permits students to decide what it is they value.
This type of instruction allows students to freely
interact with their peers and adults in a discussion of
issues that have particular importance to them. It also
provides them an opportunity to gain insight into the
fact that many values issues can be viewed differently
and can have more than one answer. Experiences of this
type add another dimension to students' value
development. Students are given the opportunity to freely
explore certain values issues in the classroom as well
as outside of school, thus providing more relevance to
their education.

WHAT ARE VALUES ALL ABOUT?

Krathwol et al. have devised a taxonomy of value development they refer to as the <u>affective domain</u>. Their classification system includes five main categories. However, for our purposes I have condensed this system into three general groups:

<u>Awareness</u>. The person is aware and responds to a stimulus in his or her environment (that is, the person is willing to attend school).

<u>Acceptance of values</u>. The person decides that school is important and makes a commitment to study.

<u>Preference for values</u>. The person has formulated a general belief that school is beneficial to him or her and he or she has integrated these attitudes into a philosophy of life.

Values are formed by our daily experiences. Therefore, it seems reasonable to assume and it has been established that people from different parts of the United States or the world have different values. It also seems reasonable that if students have modifications in their daily experiences, changes can occur in their values.

Because values mold our behavior, they are developed through extremely complex circumstances. We are placed in situations that cause us to reexamine what it is we feel is right or worth believing. Therefore, a value is not static. It is something constantly being shaped by our daily experiences.

DEVELOPING VALUES

According to Louis E. Raths et al., a person formulates a value through a valuing process that is developed through the following steps:

<u>Choosing</u>. After thoughtful consideration of the consequences of each alternative, the person must be able to select freely from a series of alternatives what he or she perceives to be good or bad.

<u>Prizing</u>. After the person makes a selection, he or she must be satisfied with it by demonstrating his or her satisfaction, thus publicly affirming his or her choice.

<u>Acting</u>. The person must act upon the choice with some repetition.

For example, let's say Sue Smith feels very strongly that everyone should strive to conserve energy. She realizes that some personal discomfort may be involved in doing this. However, she feels the other alternatives are less

satisfactory. Sue explains her position to her friends.
She also uses the public transportation system, keeps
her thermostat set at 65 degrees, and walks whenever
possible. One could say that Sue Smith has developed
the value that the energy problem is everyone's concern.

VALUES ARE PERSONAL

We have agreed that values are a result of personal
experiences and freedom of choice, and that these
experiences are influenced by the environmental conditions
in which a person lives. Someone who is reared in
Nebraska will most likely develop a different value about
"getting away from it all" than a person reared near the
Rocky Mountains. The person from Nebraska may feel free
on the open prairie, but extremely enclosed in a heavily
wooded mountain area. On the other hand, a mountain
person accustomed to living near a vast number of trees
may feel free in a wooded area, provided no other people
are nearby.

In the example cited above, it would be impossible
and unnecessary to judge which person's values are
"right." They are both derived from different frames
of reference and would be considered highly personal
choices. If we were to draw a parallel between the last
example and society, we may also gain insight into the
complexity of value development in a country such as the
United States. The United States has great geographical
differences as well as strong ethnic and cultural
variances. Add to these differences a tremendous mobility
and it becomes quite evident that people in our community
will hold different values. Because this diversity of
values exists at home and across the United States, it
seems reasonable to assume that our schools should not
be judgmental about what values their students possess.
Instead, the schools should be sensitive to the fact that
valuing is a personal, lifelong process that will continue
to be altered from childhood through adulthood. Please
do not infer from this that I believe educators should
ignore values in the classroom. This is impossible.
A teacher's attitudes and values are constantly being
shown by his or her words and actions. However, these
are the teacher's personal values and it may be possible
they are in conflict with those of his or her students.
Therefore, a teacher should be very careful not to impose
certain beliefs on his or her students. Instead, students

should be provided with value decision making experiences
and time to clarify their own value systems. Effective
teachers do this.

VALUES, MORALS, MORALITY, AND ETHICS

It may be useful, at this point, to differentiate
between the terms values, morals, morality, and
ethics. As stated before, a value is a collective term
for what a person decides is good or bad. For our
purposes, let's assume that a person's values can be
divided into two main categories: nonmoral--an evaluation
of what is good or bad with respect to objects, such as
a car, a painting, or a type of food; and moral--an
assessment of what would be considered good or bad actions
and/or motives with respect to others. Stated another
way, moral values are those that carry an obligation or
responsibility to one or more people. When a person or
a group of people decide what their moral values are,
they are then referred to as the individual's or group's
morality. In other words, morality is a collective term
for the moral values held by an individual or by a group
of individuals.

For example, murder is considered wrong by most
individuals of our society. This would appear to be a
rather easily defined moral value. However, anyone who
reads the newspaper or listens to the radio or television
is aware that much controversy surrounds this moral
value. In fact, our society has categorized this moral
value into various degrees, first degree murder being
more immoral than second or third degree murder. This
analysis or interpretation of a moral value is referred
to as the field of ethics. Ethics, then, deals with the
thinking about the degree of rightness or wrongness of
morality, moral problems, and moral decisions.

KOHLBERG'S MODEL OF MORAL DEVELOPMENT

Lawrence Kohlberg believes that a person's moral
development is a sequential process. His model consists
of three levels, each containing two stages. It is
Kohlberg's contention that a person cannot reach one stage
before experiencing a preceding one. However, this person
could operate at one stage and revert back to a lower
one in certain situations. In addition, Kohlberg's
research indicates that people in all cultures progress

through the same sequence. (Although Kohlberg does not
attach any ages to his levels, I have attempted to do
so to make these stages more useful for teachers. These
have been derived from data collected by Kohlberg in which
he has graphed the ages of the subjects he tested versus
their responses to various moral reasoning situations.
These responses were compared with the characteristics
of the following six stages to determine the level of
moral development of each person. These ages are in no
way an accurate assessment of all people and should not
be used as a guide.)

Preconventional Level: Ages 7-10. Moral decisions
    are based on self-centered needs.
    Stage I (Avoid Punishment): A person's actions
    are based on a blind obedience to avoid punishment
    or to seek a reward. The "ultimate wrong" is getting
    into trouble. Examples of Stage: (1) A child
    puts toys away so he or she may go outside to play
    with friends. (2) A child puts toys away to avoid
    being punished by parents.
    Stage II (Self-benefit): A Stage II person is
    aware of the needs and motives of others and feels
    "one good or bad turn deserves another." Examples
    of Stage: (1) A person buys a treat for a friend
    with the intention of receiving a favor in return.
    (2) The other day Jim was reprimanded by his biology
    teacher for fooling around in class. While walking
    home from school, Jim spots this teacher's car parked
    on the street. Jim decides to deflate two of the
    car's tires to get back at his teacher.
Conventional Level: Ages 10-13. Characterized by
    conformity and the maintenance of "law and order."
    Stage III (Concern for Acceptance): These
    individuals are extremely sensitive to peer
    expectations and approval. This is the first time
    that behavior is judged on the basis of intention.
    Example of Stage: (1) Susie Jones wants to go
    to the movies, but her parents say no. She in turn
    argues that "all her friends will be there."
    Stage IV (Authority Orientation): A Stage IV
    person is motivated to act according to what is
    "right" or "best" for society. His or her actions
    are highly influenced by rules, authority figures,
    and preserving social order for its own sake.
    Examples of Stage: (1) A child is told by parents

to be home at a specific time. He or she responds
to this order without question. The parents may
or may not have a good reason for demanding he or
she follow their orders, but the child's action is
based on a respect for their authority. (2) A person
is asked why he or she always drives his or her car
at the speed limit. He or she responds by saying,
"That's the law."

Postconventional Level: Ages 13-adult. Decisions are
based on values shared by others rather than
self-centered or blind interests.

Stage V (The Greatest Good for the Greatest
Number): These individuals feel that the rights
of others should be respected and that morality is
a matter of personal choice. These people feel that
laws should be changed when they no longer aid
society. Stage V people would prefer to change a
law rather than break it. However, if the
modification is not possible, they may choose to
break it and willingly suffer the consequences.
Examples of Stage: (1) Throughout the history
of our country, some young men have resisted
induction into the armed forces. They did so on
the basis that the specific war they were being
forced into was immoral. They were fully aware that
their resistance could cause them to be imprisoned.
However, they felt strongly enough about their
convictions to cause them to disobey their induction
order and suffer the consequences. (2) A student
confides in Mr. Jones about his recent involvement
in the theft of a math test. A day later in the
faculty lounge, Mr. Jones hears that three students
are going to receive a failing grade in math due
to their confessed guilt in the theft of a math
test. However, the student who confided in him was
not one of the three. Mr. Jones reasons that
revealing this student's involvement would do nothing
to develop his moral character and would completely
destroy Mr. Jones's rapport with this student.
Therefore, Mr. Jones decides to discuss this issue
with the student, but allow the student to make his
own decision regarding this matter. (In this
situation, Mr. Jones believes that a person cannot
be coerced into morality, but rather it is a matter
of a personal choice.)

Stage VI (Conscience is the Guide): Stage VI

people feel that individuality is primary to moral
decision making. "Right" is defined by a person's
conscience based on self-selected ethical principles,
such as justice, equality of human rights, and the
respect for the dignity of human beings as
individuals. <u>Examples of Stage</u>: (1) Dr. Martin
Luther King felt compelled to break some of society's
laws because he felt they were unjust in dealing
with human rights. His conscience directed him to
break these laws because he felt his actions were
consistent with certain universal ethical principles.
(2) The fathers of our country signed the Declaration
of Independence to sever the American colonies' ties
with England. This document was founded on the basis
that all men were created equal. Even though this
action was viewed by England as illegal and
punishable by death, these men refused to follow
England's laws and instead were guided by their
consciences. Their behavior was governed by specific
self-selected ethical principles.

EXPANDING KOHLBERG'S MODEL
Kohlberg has also theorized that a person's moral
development may extend into a seventh stage. In this
stage, a person would transcend from a human point of
view to a cosmic one. By this theory, a person in Stage
VII would experience life similarly to a state of being
that Abraham Maslow calls self-actualization and one that
proponents of transcendental meditation refer to as cosmic
consciousness.
To better describe the way a person in Stage VII
would view his or her existence, let's use the following
quote that explains cosmic consciousness:

the person in cosmic consciousness can make decisions
according to ultimate values rather than shortsighted
needs. . . . Sustained unbounded awareness enables
such an individual to realize a natural sense of
morality, justice, beauty, and truth, the values
projected by Maslow as the deepest level of man's
nature.

It is appropriate to point out that Kohlberg's theory
implies that there are "universal principles." Some

people disagree with this premise. However, Kohlberg's theory has utility in terms of describing human moral behavior and as a model to explain how moral behavior is acquired.

KOHLBERG'S THEORY AND AMERICAN SOCIETY

Research studies indicate that 70 percent of all Americans make most of their moral decisions based on the Stage III conventional level. Therefore, it would follow that only a minority operate from a postconventional frame of reference. It could also be stated, from these data, that the majority of moral decisions in the United States are based on conformity and the respect for authority and law and order. This should give educators a clue as to the fundamental framework that directs most of the moral decisions of their students. In addition, one could infer that if 70 percent of all Americans base their moral decisions on the conventional level, the moral development of most students never progresses past Stage IV.

Human beings have been investigating moral values for thousands of years. Out of much of the work which has been done in the area of moral values, or ethics, it is possible to develop a view of three major systems involving ethical beliefs. Although these systems do not adequately describe every unique ethical system that has been devised by people over the years, the three major groups are useful in understanding the bases upon which ethical thought lies. The three ethical system groups we will examine are identified as Principle, Consequence, and Context.

PRINCIPLE ETHICS

People who ascribe to the belief system known as principle ethics generally believe that some universal rules or norms are related to how people treat and interact with one another. This belief system was championed by such philosophers as Immanuel Kant and has had wide acceptance throughout the world. Kant developed what he called the "categorical imperative," which says, in common language, that human conduct with respect to others should be judged on the basis of whether it could serve as a universal rule for all people. Kant also advocated that people always be viewed as "ends" and never be treated as "means" to other ends. Someone operating with a system of principle ethics would contend that certain universal principles are accepted by all people (such as the value of human life, the value of truthfulness) and these serve as bases for ethical conduct. An example of principle ethics could come from the following situation:

> Rachel and Jane are good friends. Jane is dating Frank and is planning to marry him upon their graduation from high school. Last night, Rachel saw Frank out with Joan, a new girl in town. Frank and Joan were very friendly and seemed to be quite engrossed in one another. Rachel knows that telling her friend Jane of Frank's unfaithfulness will be quite painful for her, but Rachel believes it is important to tell the truth "no matter what happens." Rachel's motivation for telling Jane about Frank is based upon her use of principle ethics: namely, a rule that says honesty and truth telling regardless of the consequences is essential in her behavior as a human being.

Another example of the use of principle ethics might be the view of the person who is opposed to any abortion for any reason on the basis that "all human life is sacred and must be protected at all costs." This principle guides the ethical conduct of that person, and is another example of principle ethics.

CONSEQUENCE ETHICS

Thinkers in the 1800s, such as John Stuart Mill and Jeremy Bentham, were advocates of another system we shall call consequence ethics. They claimed that pain and pleasure were the primary motivating factors of human beings and therefore a kind of "moral calculus" could be derived. They believed that every ethical problem could be analyzed and the degree of "goodness" or "badness" of a particular action could be measured on the basis of the extent to which it provided pleasure and avoided pain. In other words, they contended that the consequences or results of actions determined their morality. The extent to which an act had consequences that increased pleasure and/or decreased pain would determine whether or not it was a moral act. The view

of "the greatest good for the greatest number" has thus
evolved into the pain-pleasure concept of contemporary
thought and is widely used in human decision making.
      Using the situation I developed earlier with Jane,
Rachel, Frank, and Joan, let's examine how consequence
ethics might apply. If Rachel is motivated by consequence
ethics, she might begin by asking herself, "What should
I do that will cause the least pain and bring the greatest
pleasure to everyone involved?" She may then reason that
to tell Jane of Frank and Joan might cause a great deal
of pain. Frank's brief interlude with Joan may have been
nothing serious and Rachel would have intervened in a
situation only to bring trouble to everyone. Frank and
Jane's relationship might be destroyed and Joan may
acquire the reputation of being someone who breaks up
relationships. Rachel may reason that Jane will
eventually be "better off" without Frank and that Frank
and Joan might be happier with each other. Using
consequence ethics, Rachel will have to "weigh the
possible outcomes of her action," and her decision will
be based upon this kind of "moral calculus."
      To use the abortion issue, a person operating with
consequence ethics might reason that an unwanted child
might cause pain and difficulty for the mother and
subsequently affect the child and hence be in favor of
an abortion as a preferred solution.

CONTEXT ETHICS
      Context ethics developed in the twentieth century
primarily out of the thinking of such people as Jean-Paul
Sartre and, more recently, Joseph Fletcher. An outgrowth
of existential philosophy, this belief system operates
under the premise that the moral value of an act can be
determined by whether a person has taken a "kind" action.
In this system, the action taken by the person in a
situation determines whether or not the act is moral.
While this sounds rather confusing, people who support
context ethics propose that moral choices only grow out
of given situations or contexts and that each situation
must be analyzed and understood to see the morality of
the actions taken. People such as Fletcher use the
dictum, "Go and do the loving thing." Often referred
to as Situation Ethics, this view has caused controversy
among people who study philosophy and ethics.
      How would Rachel operate with context ethics in her
dilemma? Rachel might reason that the situation is such

that she should do nothing until such time as she has evidence that Frank and Joan are indeed serious about one another and that Frank is two-timing Jane. She may feel that the situation at present does not merit her intervention, but that it might change and then she would. Rachel is in effect indicating that the context in which her particular problem arose demands silence at one time and action at another. She might also reason that, on the other hand, the "loving thing to do" is to tell her friend Jane about her concerns about Frank and Joan, and that as long as her own motives are pure (she is doing the loving thing), everything will turn out for the best. Both reasoning approaches would indicate the use of context ethics.

Someone examining the issue of abortion from the perspective of context ethics might react by saying, "Well, it all depends. In some cases abortion might be OK and in others it might be wrong; it would depend on the circumstances of the people involved." This person would be operating out of context ethics regarding all abortion.

We have now examined the three ethical belief systems and some examples of how they might be used by people in ethical decision making. The hypothetical situation described below and the two hypothetical responses illustrate the ethical belief system or systems the two respondents are using.

Situation 1: A 66-year-old surgeon who serves 50,000 people in a remote area needs a kidney transplant. The donor would be his 22-year-old grandson who is a promising medical student. The grandson is the father of two young children with a third on the way. Statistically it is known that on the average the donor of a kidney shortens his own life by five years. Since the "matching" of the kidneys in this particular situation is quite difficult, it is unlikely that a suitable donor for the surgeon other than the grandson will be found.

Response 1: "I think the transplant should be done. The morally right response is always to save a life. You can't play the statistics game with the grandson. An average is just that; the grandson may live an entirely normal life with no ill effects, and the surgeon grandfather can have a number of productive life-saving years ahead of him as the result."

Response 2: "If you weigh the pros and cons of this situation, I think you would have to come down on the side opposing the transplant. The grandfather is nearing the end of his career and the grandson has the potential for doing highly significant work which may benefit millions of people, not to mention the responsibilities he has to his own family."

The first response to Situation 1 indicates the person is concerned about saving human life whenever possible. This person is not weighing consequences or equivocating about situations; there is a moral principle involved and it is being applied: Save a life regardless. This person is using principle ethics. The second response to the situation shows that the person is also concerned about human life. In this instance, however, it seems that the person has decided that more good can result from not performing the operation than from making the transplant. This person is using consequence ethics.

Situation 2: A genetic counselor's services have been sought by a couple with a child who has a serious genetic defect. The parents of this child want to know what their chances are of having another child with this defect. After some examination, the counselor finds that the potential for this genetic defect is not present in the husband's genes. Since both mother and father must carry the genetic information that will cause the defect in their offspring, the counselor knows that the child with the genetic defect must have been fathered by someone other than the woman's husband. Should the counselor divulge this information to the husband?

Response 1: "I think the counselor will have to get more information on the situation regarding the couple. I think his or her professional responsibility is to tell the truth, but it has to be done in such a way as to not destroy the relationship. If he or she finds that his information may endanger the relationship, he or she should do the thing which will harm the couple the least and not tell the truth about his or her findings."

Response 2: "If I were in that situation, I'd be forced to tell the husband. As a professional, I'd be bound to maintain my integrity and honesty, regardless of the outcome. The fact that the couple seems to be interested in having more children seems to be an indication that their relationship is good, but under any circumstances, I think that knowing the truth about the situation is the only basis for any relationship."

In Response 1, the person begins by mentioning his or her regard for the principle of truth telling, but then goes on to conclude that the proper decision should be based partly upon another principle: namely, that human relationships should not knowingly be destroyed or jeopardized. This person's statement that the action that will harm the couple the least might be alternatively interpreted as being either consequence ethics or context ethics. I believe this is a complex response, but it probably shows context ethics to be most operative in this person's thinking.

The second response seems to be more clear-cut. The person apparently values the principles of integrity, professional honesty, and truth telling, and justifies the use of principle ethics by stating that truth is the only basis for a relationship.

These example situations should have provided a better grasp of the three ethical belief systems. Although it may appear that this type of analysis is difficult, it is possible to acquire more skill in understanding the perspectives of students by understanding this type of model. But it is important to recognize that this is a model only, not ethical behavior in actuality. This model, as others I have presented earlier, should be seen as helps to you in organizing your thinking about your students' moral, ethical, and value behaviors. Don't try to force their positions or views into one of the three of these systems. Rather, try to distinguish consistencies, inconsistencies, and the complicated combinations of belief systems that people employ as they work through moral problems.

Whenever choices related to other people are made, ethical belief systems are employed. Certainly people in real life situations use combinations and/or bits and pieces of all three systems to justify their actions. It would be unwise to suppose that personal consistency is an important criteria for assessing someone's morality. Nevertheless, our ethical belief systems, examined or unexamined, do influence how we make moral decisions. It follows then that whenever people having differing ethical belief systems investigate a problem involving moral values, they may conflict or clash regarding the proper decision.

Each of the three ethical systems has its difficulties in certain situations and no single system can be rationally preferred over the other. Those who employ principle ethics often find themselves in situations in which two or more of their principles are in conflict. Those who advocate consequence ethics often cannot clearly identify the decision that will provide the greatest pleasure and the least pain. People adopting a position based upon situation, or context, ethics are often forced to conclude that the "loving thing to do" cannot be determined absolutely. Because people generally are unaware of their ethical belief systems, and because these systems all possess inadequacies, controversy over moral questions is practically assured.

When teachers are involved in classroom sessions that deal with questions involving moral values, it is important they recognize the belief systems being used by their students and by themselves. When belief systems conflict, the major premises used in the discussion are in conflict. Under such circumstances, "right" or "wrong" decisions are tied to the different premises and belief systems. Helping students to understand that their premises and belief systems are in conflict is an important first step in understanding the nature of the problem. In classroom situations dealing with moral values, the goal should be one of developing an understanding of the differing premises causing the controversy of values and not one of resolving the controversy. If teachers can do this effectively, they will be encouraging rational analysis of problems and will be developing a spirit of tolerance among their students. To disagree with someone else is not "bad" provided we know why we are in disagreement!

NONMORAL VALUES

Many factors in society influence our nonmoral values. As we experience life, we adopt goals, adapt to our environmental surroundings, and make many decisions relative to our nonmoral values. Economics, cultural norms, politics, geography, and religion will influence our decision making. As teachers select topics and issues for classroom interaction, their knowledge of how societal factors influence the valuing processes of students is crucial in understanding how to choose and facilitate an effective learning session.

Economics

America is a mass of economic complexity. Probably the vast majority of problems, issues, and decisions relative to them are influenced heavily by economic considerations. The economic activity in an area can, to a large extent, determine whether a particular issue or topic will be controversial. Many nonmoral values are related to economics where the emphasis is on the value of materials and services. Often nonmoral values come into conflict because of economic considerations related to them.

As an example, let's consider a situation in which the Environmental Protection Agency (EPA) has investigated air pollution in a small community and has ruled that the single large industry in town is polluting the air and must either come into compliance with federal clean air standards or shut down.

Economically, the plant may not have a sufficient base to bring its operation up to federal standards. If the plant shuts down, the economy of the town will be destroyed, people will be unable to find employment, and financial disaster for everyone in the town will be imminent. While most people in the community probably value clean air and would even support federal efforts to maintain it, the EPA ruling becomes quite controversial in the community as it becomes apparent that economic hardship will result from the action. A classroom activity on air pollution in this town poses much more potential controversy than it would in other areas where the local economic problem does not exist.

Similarly, the people in a town adjacent to a large military base may value cutbacks in government spending. However, when the Department of Defense decides to abandon the military base, the value of financial security quickly takes precedent over the prior value. Finally, a teacher in a health class may decide to teach a unit on the health hazards associated with smoking. While most people value health quite highly, this teacher quickly becomes

embroiled in a local controversy because he or she is
teaching in an agricultural area where the main product
is cigarette tobacco.

All of these examples point out the extent to which
economic considerations influence our nonmoral values.
It may be that some of the most significant problems in
our society today are centered around conflicting nonmoral
values and teachers who can facilitate constructive study
of such problems are certain to be successful in educating
their students for the future.

Cultural Norms

The standards or norms of a culture are taught to
children throughout their lives. In adolescence, societal
norms are often challenged by the norms of the teenage
subculture, but overall, the nonmoral values of people
are adjusted by experiences resulting from living in a
culture that has developed certain ways of solving
problems and acting. The so-called "work ethic," which
seems to permeate most of American culture, has been under
fire for years. Yet most American still value work and
react negatively to others who do not.

The American culture has also come to value private
transportation. The automobile has become such an
integral part of our lives that life without it is
unthinkable. While the cultural norm may dictate the
two-car or three-car family, there is a growing
realization that this value is in conflict with other
such values as wise use of resources, conservation of
energy, clean air, and a safer life.

The values of the population as a whole, as
characterized and inferred from its collective actions
and behaviors, provides an excellent background against
which students can thoughtfully examine their personal
values. The social changes that typify contemporary life
are bound to generate conflict and controversy. Areas
of social change that relate to nonmoral values can and
should be distinguished from areas relating to moral
values.

Gay rights, civil liberties, social welfare, and
single-parent families are among the examples of moral
value issues presently in conflict with cultural norms.
Many of the moral values of our culture are being
questioned and examined today in an effort to discern
whether the reasons for their development were legitimate,

and if so, whether they are justifiable now. Students may either accept or reject various cultural moral values, and how they react to them can influence how they will respond in class settings relative to nonmoral cultural values. In working with students, teachers can recognize the distinction between nonmoral and moral cultural norms related to issues, and recall that differing premises result in differing conclusions, or result in the same conclusion but for differing reasons.

Politics

Many teachers feel that such topics as democracy, socialism, communism, and totalitarianism should never be discussed in the classroom. Political ideologies can and do influence people's values, often in paradoxical and inconsistent relation to other values they hold. The political inclinations of a community may influence controversial issues in classroom discussions. Popular political figures who have taken a position on a nonmoral or moral issue may influence the values of the rest of the population. Other issues often are associated with various political ideologies and this "guilt by association" can result in confused discussion on the part of students who are investigating the problem. It is necessary for teachers to understand the political influences operating in the community as they approach topics that may have been aligned with other ideological views. As before, being able to help students distinguish between the components inherent in an issue and extraneous "baggage" carried along in the debate surrounding the issue is important for successful instruction and learning.

Geography and Ethnicity

America is not the "great melting pot" people once thought it to be. Ethnic origins and cultural differences have interacted with the geography of the United States to produce a highly diversified nation. The immigrant groups who settled the country collected in certain geographic localities throughout the country, bringing their cultural values and ethics with them. Two hundred years later, or less, many of the ethnic imports have remained to provide a rich base of values. The geographic area in which you teach will have its own unique ethnic flavor that will be part of the students' values repertoire. The interaction of the ethnic component with

the geographic conditions of the country has resulted
in a unique blend of views and life-styles that must be
discerned in order to understand the students and to
facilitate their education in the areas of values and
controversial issues.

Religion

Along with other components of ethnic heritage,
people brought their religious belief systems with them
as they came to America. Religious beliefs are extremely
powerful forces in the development of students' values.
A lack of awareness of the religious traditions and
beliefs of the students in the classroom can be
embarrassing to teachers as they engage in discussions
of controversial topics. Even noncontroversial areas
can be potential problems for the teacher when religious
values and beliefs are not recognized or understood by
him or her.

VALUES EDUCATION AND THE SCHOOLS

According to a 1976 Gallup Poll, values education
is favored by four out of five Americans. However, the
term values education has different meanings for
different people. Some individuals view values education
as the instilling of specific values into students, while
others see it as a process in which students examine their
beliefs and formulate their own judgments on specific
moral and nonmoral decisions.

Douglas Superka et al. have compiled an overview
of the primary values education approaches used in
American schools. This overview is as follows:

1. Inculcation
    Purposes: To instill or internalize certain values
    in students; to change the values of students so they
    more nearly reflect certain desired values.
    Methods: Modeling, positive and negative
    reinforcement, mocking, nagging, manipulating
    alternatives, providing incomplete or biased data,
    games and simulations, role playing, discovery
    learning.
2. Moral Development
    Purposes: To help students develop more complex
    moral reasoning patterns based on a higher set of
    values; to urge students to discuss the reasons for

their value choices and positions, not merely to share with others, but to foster change in the stages of reasoning of students.

Methods: Moral dilemma episodes, with the small-group discussion being relatively structured and argumentative.

3. Clarification

Purposes: To help students become aware of and identify their own values and those of others; to help students communicate openly and honestly with others about their values; to help students use both rational thinking and emotional awareness to examine their personal feelings, values, and behavior patterns.

Methods: Role playing games, simulations, contrived or real value-laden situations, in-depth self-analysis exercises, sensitivity activities, out-of-class activities, small-group discussion.

4. Action Learning

Purposes: Those purposes listed for analysis and clarification; to provide students with opportunities for personal and social action based on their values; to encourage students to view themselves as socially interactive beings, not fully autonomous, but members of a community or social system.

Methods: The methods listed for analysis and clarification as well as action projects within the school and community and skill practice in group organizing and interpersonal relations.

5. Analysis

Purposes: To help students use logical thinking and scientific investigation to decide value issues and questions; to help students use rational, analytical processes in interrelating and conceptualizing their values.

Methods: Structured rational discussion that demands the application of reasons as well as evidence, testing principles, analyzing analogous cases, debate, and research.

HOW DO TEACHERS FEEL ABOUT VALUES EDUCATION?

To assess teachers' attitudes about values education, I have included the following self-evaluation. This exercise gives some insight into which values education

approach(es) they believe is/are appropriate for the
classroom.
     Indicate "Agree," "Disagree," or "Not sure" opposite
the following statements. Check the appropriate space
on the right.

		Agree	Disagree	Not sure
I believe a values education approach should help students:				
1.	Become aware of their own values	_____	_____	_____
2.	Change their values in some cases, so they more clearly reflect society's values	_____	_____	_____
3.	Act on their values	_____	_____	_____
4.	Use logical thinking in decision making	_____	_____	_____
5.	Interact with one another to discuss reasons for their value choices	_____	_____	_____
6.	Instill positive values in each other	_____	_____	_____
7.	Develop more complex moral reasoning patterns	_____	_____	_____
8.	Communicate openly and honestly with others regarding their values	_____	_____	_____
9.	Use rational thought and emotions to examine their feelings and values	_____	_____	_____
10.	Critically analyze their values	_____	_____	_____

HOW TO INTERPRET THE SELF-EVALUATION
     Agreeing or being not sure about the following items
indicates that you either tend to favor the following

values education approaches or have not completely
developed your philosophy regarding these approaches.

1, 3, 5, 8, and 9	Clarification
2 and 6	Inculcation
3 and 8	Action learning
4 and 10	Analysis
5 and 7	Moral development

If a teacher disagrees with all ten statements, he
or she either does not favor these values education
approaches or does not want to incorporate values
education into the curriculum.

SOME VALUES EDUCATION RESEARCH
        Some interesting research findings indicate a lack
of values education may be producing a society of
individuals incapable of determining certain acts as being
unethical. For example, Kurt and Gladys Lang at New York
University and Amitai Etzioni at Columbia University gave
a similar questionnaire dealing with the ability to rank
unethical behavior to some of the their undergraduate
students. The students could identify a behavior, such
as one person stealing from another, as unethical.
However, when the behavior dealt with an institution,
such as one person cheating on income taxes, they were
generally unable to recognize this act as being equally
wrong. These data imply some deplorable future scenarios.
        Another informal study in this area tends to reveal
why some students are incapable of determining whether
certain acts are unethical. Iozzi and Lockley, at Rutgers
University, as reported by Etzioni, found that students
majoring in the humanities tend to reason at higher moral
levels than those in the sciences. If we assume that
Rutgers students are similar to most students in the
United States, one may infer that science is one
discipline that has primarily concentrated on cognitive
and psychomotor skills rather than on issues in the
affective domain.
        Earlier in this chapter it was mentioned that a
person's values were formulated through daily experiences.
It was stated that people continually modify their values
by being placed in situations that tend to conflict with
their existing behavior patterns. If we accept this basic

assumption regarding values and valuing, it would seem logical that an important function of education should be to give students time to examine their beliefs and to sort out what it is they value as good or bad. By allowing students to make decisions concerning their values, educators can also provide experiences that will foster logical reasoning and critical thinking.

WHY SOME EDUCATORS FAVOR MORAL DEVELOPMENT AND CLARIFICATION

Lawrence Kohlberg, mentioned before as to his model of moral development, is a leading proponent of using the "moral dilemma" or moral development approach with students. Through this technique, students are not inculcated with certain values but are able to actively examine their own values and those of their peers by being confronted with the situation described before: "What Would You Do?"

A genetic counselor's services have been sought by a couple who have a child with a serious genetic defect. The parents want to know their chances of having another child with the same defect. After some examination, the counselor finds that the genetic defect is not present in the husband's genes. Since both mother and father must carry the genetic information that will cause the defect in their offspring, the counselor knows that the child with the genetic defect must have been fathered by someone other than the husband. Should the counselor divulge this information to the husband? (This particular example may not be appropriate for use in your classroom. Discretion must be exercised as to the type of moral dilemmas and/or moral issues that you present in your instruction.)

Kohlberg and others claim that by presenting moral dilemmas in classroom instruction, they have helped students in raising their moral reasoning by one level, based on Kohlberg's model for moral development.

Kohlberg also believes that moral development is influenced by a person's religious background. However, he feels that it is possible to assist moral growth independent of religious education.

Advocates of clarification appear to hold generally the same antiinculcation philosophy as those favoring moral dilemmas. The difference is that they construct

their activities with the main purpose of assisting
students in developing the "valuing process."
    An example of this approach is as follows:

                    Electricity and You
List ten electrical appliances you or your family use
at home.

1.	6.
2.	7.
3.	8.
4.	9.
5.	10.

Circle those you feel you or your family could do without.
1. How many appliances on your list are essential for
    you and your family?
2. Make an attempt for one week to live without the
    electrical items you circled on your list. Keep a
    record of your progress for each day. Time will be
    allotted for you to share your list with others in
    class.

    According to Sidney B. Simon et al., leaders of the
clarification approach, students exposed to clarification
techniques are able to critically analyze problems better
than those not exposed to clarification activities. They
also contend that the students who have been introduced
to the clarification approach have demonstrated the
ability to follow through on their decisions. In other
words, clarification has been shown to be an effective
strategy in developing better decision makers.
    Moral development, clarification, analysis, and
action learning are all similar philosophically. By using
moral development and clarification activities, students
have the opportunity to analyze their values and act in
accordance with their beliefs.
    Allowing students to examine their own beliefs is
far more pragmatic than attempting to instill them with
the values of someone else. For example, schools may
attempt to teach that drinking alcohol at an illegal age
is wrong. However, there is sufficient evidence to
demonstrate that this will do very little to stop the
underage consumption of alcohol. As one study indicates,
peer pressure has the greatest influence on the alcohol
drinking behavior of adolescents.
    When students are not in school, they formulate their

own values by the experiences of their own environment,
which includes the interaction they encounter with their
peers. Giving them this opportunity in school may add
tremendous relevance to their education. Therefore,
teachers should try all the values education approaches
listed earlier except inculcation.

SOME SUGGESTIONS REGARDING VALUES EDUCATION
     Some suggestions about the use of values education
approaches are included below, along with some examples
and specific suggestions.

1. Create a classroom environment of trust. If the
    students feel they can respond freely and openly,
    they will tend to answer more honestly. (This type
    of environment does not occur overnight. Be patient!)
    Example: If a student professes to believe in
    racial discrimination, do not inform the student that
    his convictions are wrong even though his statements
    may not agree with your beliefs. You can ask for
    other comments on this subject, but again be careful
    not to force your beliefs on the students. With
    differing views on a specific subject, students may
    be confronted with logical inconsistencies in their
    thought patterns. It is the intention of four of
    the five values education approaches (moral
    development, clarification, action learning, and
    analysis) to allow students to consider freely their
    own beliefs and to make choices freely on the basis
    of these considerations.
2. Make an all-out effort not to judge the responses
    of the students. It may be helpful at times to
    clarify their answers and comments, but refrain from
    offering your opinion unless you are asked for it.
    Example: A student may say that he feels that
    abortion is wrong. You might respond to the student
    by saying, "Why do you feel this technique is wrong?"
    Or, you may say, "Do you feel abortion is wrong in
    all circumstances?"
3. If you feel you must give your opinion on an issue,
    be sure you make it very clear that "this is my
    opinion." Example: Student: "What do you think,
    Miss Jones?" Miss Jones: "If you want to know my
    opinion, I believe that it is impossible to pass

general legislation to deal with certain issues. Therefore, people must decide for themselves whether they want to accept abortion or not."

4. Be a good listener. To encourage student responses, you must be willing to listen carefully to all of the students.

5. Develop activities and experiences of personal and social concern to the students. If a student feels the subject discussed is highly personal, respect his or her right not to respond.

6. Use divergent questioning whenever possible. Such questions permit open-ended responses, thereby encouraging a wider variety of student interaction. Example: "What do you think are some of the ethical problems that a totally implantable artificial heart (TIAH) may pose to our society?" This type of question allows for many possible responses and can be contrasted with the following convergent question that tends to limit a person's answer: "What does Dr. Christiaan Barnard say about the effectiveness of the TIAH?"

7. If the values activity requires student interaction, allow enough time for the sharing of views.

8. Try to foster the type of environment in which students can affirm their convictions without belittling the views of others. Example: If a student responds to one of his or her classmates in the following way: "That was really a stupid answer!" it is important to point out that you want your classroom environment to operate on the basis of mutual respect. Therefore, if a student wishes someone to respect his or her opinions, he or she must respect others' opinions also.

9. Develop the distinction between respect for an opinion (acceptance of a person's right to hold a belief or opinion) and agreement with an opinion. While teachers need to respect student opinions, they certainly do not have to agree with them!

10. Students may perceive that their personal convictions are being attacked by either you or their peers even though you are nonjudgmental of all comments or views. If this does occur, create situations for students to explain their feelings regarding the topics that caused the personal conflicts. This may help students recognize that their attitudes

were so strong about specific issues that contradictions to their logic may have been misconstrued as personal attacks.

REFERENCES AND SUGGESTED READINGS

Barman, Charles R., and Rusch, John J. "A Case For Bioethics in the Secondary Curriculum." School, Science and Mathematics, 78(1) (January 1978): 3-8.

Barman, Charles R.; Rusch, John J.; Cooney, Timothy M. Science and Societal Issues: A Guide For Science Teachers. Ames, Iowa: Iowa State University Press, 1981.

Beauchamp, T. L., and Walters, LeRoy, eds. Bioethics. Belmont, Calif.: Dickenson, 1978.

Beecher, Henry K. Research and the Individual. Boston: Little, Brown, 1970.

Etzioni, Amitai, "Should Schools Add 'Moral Education' to Their Curricula?" Minneapolis Tribune, October 17, 1976.

Kohlberg, Lawrence, Developmental Psychology Today. Del Mar, Calif.: CRM Books, 1974.

Krathwol, David, et al. Taxonomy of Educational Objectives, The Classification of Educational Goals, Handbook II: Affective Domain. New York: David McKay, 1964.

Morrison, Eleanor S., and Price, Mila Underhill. Values in Sexuality. New York: Hart, 1974.

Potter, Van Rensselaer. Bioethics: Bridge to the Future. Englewood Cliffs, N. J.: Prentice-Hall, 1971.

Raths, Louis E., et al. Values and Teaching. Columbus, Ohio: Charles E. Merrill, 1966.

Simon, Sidney B., et al. Values Clarification. New York: Hart, 1972.

Superka, Douglas P., et al. Values Education: Approaches and Materials. Boulder, Colo.: Social Science Education Consortium, 1975.

3

LEARNING THROUGH HUMANISTIC EDUCATION

Richard F. Strub

Humanistic education focuses on helping students recognize their own potential, clarify their worth as individuals, and set personal short-range and long-range goals. It is the learning of life skills--those that relate to the development of a humane world view.

Along with cognitive education, humanistic teachers emphasize affective education, education which relates to the feeling or emotional aspect of experience and learning. It refers to how students feel about wanting to learn, how they feel as they learn, and what they feel afterward.

Gloria Castillo identifies the affective side of learning as the emotional part of the educational experience, just as the cognitive domain is the intellectual part. Effective teachers are able to make each interrelate. The interrelationships are recognized as the cognitive domain stimulates the affective domain and the student becomes involved in affective experiences.

RATIONALE FOR HUMANISTIC TEACHING

I have found more and more teachers accepting the reality of the relationship between the cognitive and affective areas of functioning. How students feel about themselves as persons and as learners relates closely to their involvement in the learning process and how they relate to others in the educational setting. In curricula that are often information-oriented, effective teachers are increasingly accepting the importance of the self.

In a contemporary period of confusion and change, educators must help young people explore their roles as

individuals who are growing and changing. They need
assistance in understanding how they make friends and
relate to them as well as how they interact within social
groups. Opportunities are needed for them to examine
how they treat people different from themselves, and how
they synthesize personal interests and desires with what
is best for the social good. Given these and similar
experiences, young people are better able to shape their
own identity and personal character and may become
positive contributors to society.

In humanistic instruction, the teacher tries to
understand how the students view themselves. The students
are seen as unique persons who achieve self-development
through contact with others. They are aware of
themselves, and are capable of making choices that guide
their behavior.

The positive potentialities of people to change and
grow as individuals is emphasized strongly. An important
goal of humanistic education is to help each student
become the best human being possible, with the focus on
maximum development as a fully functioning and integrated
individual. The concepts of love, intimacy, creativity,
warmth, and honesty are given careful attention in
humanistic education.

The 1971 White House Conference on Children
recognized the importance of humanism when the delegates
voted as the top two priorities, as identified by K. Close
to:

1.   Provide opportunities for every child to learn, grow,
     and live creatively by reordering national priorities.
2.   Redesign education to achieve individualized,
     humanized, child-centered learning.

Living is a skill and good teachers are needed to
foster the personal and social growth of their students
directly by allowing for learning opportunities that offer
practice in such areas as decision making, effective
communication, and understanding of self and others.
Effective teachers usually aid young people in learning
to be human by behaving humanly toward them.

HELPING STUDENTS DEVELOP POSITIVE SELF-CONCEPTS
     We did not inherit our self-concept. It is learned.
We begin to gain information about ourselves and our world

at the earliest moments of life. Just as we are constantly receiving new impressions and ideas relative to our personal needs and desires, we are gradually forming new impressions and attitudes about ourselves.

There is little challenge to the concept that young people need sufficient confidence in themselves and their ability to succeed before they will learn in the school setting. A person's concept of self and his or her efforts to have control over his or her environment and future destiny have a very direct relationship. The stronger the students feel about their self-worth, the greater the possibility that they will be motivated to learn and have control over their social behavior.

Educators have considerable impacts on how students see themselves as learners in the classroom. As significant adults in the lives of these young people, teachers' behavior has much to do with the opinions and attitudes students form. In being with students, a process forms that will leave a great impression on whether students see themselves as successful—persons with potential. This potential can last beyond the classroom and the present; it rather represents the future and success there also. This optimistic approach to learning implies that the teacher must see something in the learner that the learner does not see in himself or herself.

As teachers gain additional understanding of self-concept and how it relates to learning, they will enhance the atmosphere of their classrooms greatly by reducing student disruption, apathy, inattention, and other common management problems.

Disruptive students have learned to see themselves as troublemakers and behave accordingly. The self-concept doesn't cause the undesirable behavior, but it tends to guide and influence the direction or form of behavior that the student exhibits. If the individual sees himself or herself as a "bad kid," he or she will display "bad kid" behavior.

The formation of an individual's self-concept is a complex, continuous process but it can be noted optimistically that change is possible. As significant adults in the lives of students, teachers can have a positive effect on this change by influencing them to think well of themselves and their potential to learn. Teachers have a responsibility to respect the psychological growth young people need to make as their new ideas and impressions of self filter into their consciousness. While we are certain to encounter students who have negative feelings and impressions about themselves that will have a definite effect on their classroom behavior and motivation, we must maintain optimism about the potential for change. We should not, in any way, contribute to a student's negative self-concept by giving him or her another opportunity to say, "Here is one more adult who thinks I'm no good," or, "who doesn't care."

The directions students take are greatly influenced by the beliefs held about them as individuals. If teachers take the position that certain students in the class cannot gain from instruction or have little potential for learning, it is unlikely that teachers will succeed in motivating them to learn. Young people are going to develop best if they are seen as individuals who hold relatively untapped potential and if they are continually encouraged to realize this potential. The teacher's responsibility is to behave in ways that invite students' positive, emotional reactions regarding themselves and their abilities.

Teachers can influence change in the self-concepts of students by holding positive, definite expectations for each of them. A confident self-concept on the part of the teacher, moreover, conveys that the teacher has something important to share with the students and he or she fully expects them to become involved. If teachers create an atmosphere of definite expectations they are communicating to students that they have confidence in them as learners and their ability to assume responsibility. A fine line must be drawn between the teachers' standards and students' goals in achieving at a level higher than they think they can accomplish. Establishing definite teacher expectations relative to achievement, behavior, and values of each student encourages a strong sense of student self-worth.

Many of us have gone into teaching because of one or more teachers who made an exceptional impression on us. That impression likely was related to the way those teachers communicated to us a sense of caring. We were made to feel important; he or she reinforced our sense of self-worth. Conversely, most of us can also recall someone who humiliated us in front of our classmates by ridiculing or putting us down. Typically, those teachers made our school experience negative. As teachers, we have the power to have strong impact on the self-concepts of our students each and every day that we teach. The choice is ours.

CREATING A PLEASURABLE AND POSITIVE ENVIRONMENT FOR LEARNING

It makes sense that pleasurable learning in a pleasurable environment lasts longer and has more influence on subsequent behavior. Learning can and should come about as a result of positive experiences.

Benjamin Bloom and fellow researchers discovered that most students achieve similar learning ability, learning rate, and desire for additional learning when they are placed in a favorable learning environment. When students are placed in unfavorable conditions, these learning qualities become much less similar.

All the ideas presented here work indirectly to promote achievement in academic subjects. Developing strong self-concepts, focusing on self-awareness, creating a positive learning environment, developing interpersonal communication skills, and establishing positive school morale can be said to be keys to cognitive skill development. Traditional teacher training programs and teaching styles often give teachers the feeling that time spent in humanistic or affective education activities could better be used in getting to the cognitive aspects of the course. However, the time spent in improving the learning environment or the motivational atmosphere of a classroom is most likely to be time well invested. It is clear that well-motivated students in a pleasant setting learn more and at a faster rate than those whose level of motivation is obstructed or reduced due to an unfavorable, negative psychological classroom atmosphere.

None of us, whether student or adult, feels much responsibility for things over which we have no control. A classroom should have structure but the environment should allow the students some opportunity to define their own structure always within limits. Students don't want or need license, rather they need to know that the classroom is a safe place where they are encouraged to try out their reasoning and thinking skills. This freedom is needed and desirable, and with it comes responsibility. The school setting is a large part of a student's world

and, therefore, it is necessary to give them some of the
responsibility for creating that world. Learning the
concept, "I am in control of myself," goes a long way
in developing responsible people who accept the idea that
they control their own destiny. When students are
encouraged to make important choices in their daily lives,
it is certainly more likely that they will be able to
sort out the significant factors in decision making
situations.

Because of their direct relationship to the learning
environment, interpersonal skills that support active
cooperation in problem solving and those needed for
working out conflicts between individuals, need to receive
focus from teachers whenever possible. These skills are
not unique to any one subject matter area--all classes
need to be concerned with those skills that emphasize
the ability to appreciate and build on the efforts of
others; the ability to be an active listener, and to give
empathy to another person in time of need. Giving and
receiving useful feedback as well as the ability to both
seek and give direction are qualities to be emphasized
at several levels of development in youth. Think of the
potential for improving interpersonal relationships if
we are successful in developing those qualities that
permit students to trust others and to elicit trust from
others. We should consider also the potential for good
when we aid students in developing the ability to use
group planning as a cooperative, strengthening power
rather than as a competitive, divisive force.

An important consideration often overlooked in trying
to create a positive learning environment for students
is the physical arrangement of the classroom. Many of
us are not conscious of what the space in our classroom
reflects about ourselves. It is important that teachers
examine the physical environment of their classrooms and
determine what can be done to make it a more pleasant
and warmer place for learning. A thoughtful arrangement
of desks or tables can do much to create an atmosphere
of community as compared to the more frequently found
sterile settings. Teachers who want to be less
authoritarian must work in open and creative ways to
establish this atmosphere.

When I think back to my elementary as well as high
school classes and the rooms I took those classes in,
the first thing I recall are the sterile and formal
settings, all desks in straight rows and the teacher's

desk at the front of the room. Putting the desks or tables in a circle or in clusters so students could see each other's faces as we discussed a topic was never thought of.

There is no one correct way of handling the spacial organization in our classrooms. Rather, we need to be flexible, letting the environment reflect what we are doing in the classroom at a particular time, always allowing for the introduction of new experiences and new discoveries. Teachers might wish to make a paper mockup of the room and reposition experimentally the furniture in the available space. Perhaps an important consideration to keep in mind as we examine the physical setting of our classrooms relates to the effect a particular environment will have on how students participate.

Some additional suggestions to teachers for creating a positive learning environment are:

1. Occasionally give students some time for quiet thinking or reflecting by allowing them to daydream, doodle, draw, or listen to soft music for a short time.
2. Reduce tensions by diminishing the factors that create them, such as intense competition, fear of failure, or trying to live up to a false set of standards.
3. Use teaching techniques or strategies that allow students a genuine chance for success and a chance to discover and correct their mistakes without feeling inadequate or inferior.
4. Occasionally give students the opportunity to study or investigate something of very real interest to them--an area of study that permits them to become genuinely involved.
5. Create opportunities that involve the learner in planning, implementing, and evaluating many of the educational experiences they will have.
6. Always strive for the respect and dignity of all students. This can best be accomplished by dealing with students as individuals, giving them a feeling of being worthwhile, and able to contribute to and be a part of society.
7. Try to discover what your students feel and what they think about when they aren't forced to think about school subjects.

8. Teachers must learn to work in open and creative ways themselves if they want their classrooms to become less authoritarian and more positive centers for creative learning.
9. Many of the classroom management or control problems that face teachers could be greatly improved if these same teachers would see students in essentially positive ways and then encourage them to behave accordingly. Like most of us, students benefit greatly from others who see and communicate to them the positive traits and potentials they may not see in themselves.

PERSONAL CHARACTERISTICS OF HUMANE TEACHERS

Nothing classroom teachers do will be more important to the climate of the classroom than the emotional atmosphere they establish. The attitudes the teacher and the students have relative to themselves and each other have a tremendous effect on the learning climate.

No matter what the setting, traditional, conservative, or liberal, teachers must manage that environment in one way or another. We each want to think our management style is uniquely our own. However, many of us have adopted our styles of classroom management by accident, imitation, or emotion rather than by careful examination and selection of alternatives. In the classroom and in other dealings with students, teachers must be careful not to permit small infractions to irritate them and grow into feelings of resentment and hostility. Hostile feelings build into lasting resentment and a powerfully negative atmosphere will permeate the classroom if the irritating incidents that cause them are not dealt with as they occur. Openly sharing feelings with the students who are causing the irritations can be very difficult under the pressures of the situation and in the presence of other students. Many times teachers either explode emotionally in this situation and put the student down in some way or they ignore the behavior and allow the resentment to build. But, positive student-teacher confrontation in which the teacher models an attitude of respect can lead to open communication between the teacher and the student. In this atmosphere, compromise and negotiation can be used to solve interpersonal relationship conflicts. There is little doubt, however, that this approach to confrontation in the school setting represents a real change for many teachers and would necessitate considerable practice for them.

In most situations where confrontation between student and teacher develops as a result of student behavior, meaningful communication usually breaks down because the teacher continually tells the student what is wrong with his or her behavior rather than explaining how the teacher is feeling in the situation. When teachers tell a student what is wrong with him or her, they quickly put him or her on the defensive. They are sending "you" messages to the student with this approach and they almost invariably "blame" the student for something--"you are wrong; you know better than that; you are upsetting the class." Usually, little understanding and empathy is communicated in these messages. Typically the result is bitterness and hostility on the part of the recipient of such a message. "I" messages, on the other hand, usually share personal facts regarding the teacher's feelings. There is less likely to be the antagonism developed in statements that say, "I am very upset right now; I am becoming angry with what is happening; I am feeling very disappointed," when compared with what is conveyed in the conflict-laden "you" messages. This small change in the teacher's approach to communicating with others can pay big dividends in the relationships with them.

If a teacher needs more information to be convinced of the rationale for this approach to handling classroom irritations, perhaps it would be valuable to occasionally reflect back in time and recall his or her days in school. Effective, helpful teachers invariably possess an ability to understand and empathize with the students they come in contact with. We all were at one time the age of our students and it is valuable for us to reflect on the confusions, frustrations, concerns, and feelings that young people of this age so often encounter.

Added to the qualities already stated, other characteristics of the humanistic teacher are:

1. Alert in the classroom to expressions that communicate deep or strong feelings, and tries to understand these emotions from the student's point of view.

2. Aware that he or she has a major influence on the emotional mood or climate of the classroom learning environment.
3. Allows for one-to-one contacts with individual students; these subtle but important contacts are exceptionally important for shy, withdrawn students who are sometimes ignored.
4. Aware of self. It is important to be able to recognize not only beliefs, attitudes, values, and feelings in general, but to understand how recent experiences or happenings influence a teacher's behavior and reactions toward students.
5. Models openness by sharing feelings and thoughts. This technique is used not in a manner that imposes values or demands on the group but in a way that communicates to the students that they may or may not accept them.
6. Recognizes their own limitations as well as their strengths. Knowing prejudices, suspicions, and other imperfections is an important first step in making changes in a teaching style.
7. Are continually seeking new or additional methods to facilitate learning in their classroom. Varying the teaching style and using different techniques for communicating with the students can ignite a spark of enthusiasm for learning in some previously uncommitted young person.
8. Actively listens to students when they talk, thus communicating a strong sense of caring. In addition to listening with our ears, we need to use our eyes for contact with the other person. The position that we take with our body in some situations can communicate much about the degree of interest and caring we have relative to this person.
9. Develops a teaching style that is genuine, as described by noted psychologist Carl Rogers. The way that we communicate, interact, praise, or teach should be real, not phony. We continually need to strive for credibility and honesty in our relationships.
10. Gives the student a feeling of being able to contribute to the school, community, and society in general. A sense of worth and dignity is communicated to all students because they are treated as individuals. Students are met and dealt with

where they are presently functioning, intellectually, socially, and emotionally.

11. Fosters a sense of awareness on the part of their students; awareness focuses on the here-and-now, helping the student become conscious of his or her total living self as it relates to others and the environment. It enables the student to identify with something larger than self: others in the world.

12. Typically involves learners in planning, implementing, and to some extent, evaluating their own educational experiences. In so doing, students are able to relate to the learning activities in a lasting and more meaningful way.

KNOWING OURSELVES

Perhaps the most difficult and threatening human experience is examining and knowing one's self. As teachers try to make schools better places for students to be, they are going to have to look realistically at their own behavior and their own potential. This is not easy because since they began training for their careers they have been taught how to evaluate and observe others, not themselves. It is, however, a most necessary step if they are to function so that students develop maximum potential.

Self-knowledge leads to a less distorted perception of reality, with greater freedom and creativity as a result. As educators, we must continually struggle to gain an understanding of the processes that affect our feelings, thoughts, goals, and behaviors, thus allowing us to be free for the development of our best potentialities. Self-understanding will allow us to relate to and understand others more effectively. The better we know ourselves the better we should be able to control our environment and our emotions. Increased self-knowledge enables us to be more deliberate, more intentional in our responses to those things going on around us.

Like all people, teachers have untapped potential; if these potentials are allowed to be expressed, a tremendous personal growth is the result. Too many times we see people proceed through their lives responding with the same set of emotions to the same stimuli time after time.

The same things continue to upset, anger, frighten, and
please them. They don't seem to be able to change their
predictable, unsatisfying, habitual responses.

An important first step in self-understanding and
control is when we can predict our reactions. We need
to know what makes us angry, frustrated, nervous, or
anxious as well as those situations that create positive
reactions such as happiness and fulfillment in our
teaching. The knowledge and understanding of what brings
about unsatisfying negative responses on our part will
permit us to go on to the next important step of
developing alternative responses. Awareness and insight
are important but are not enough. If we experiment and
evaluate alternative responses to some of our less
satisfying past behaviors, we can determine whether or
not we wish to replace the old behaviors or reactions
with the new alternatives.

CONTRIBUTING TO A MORE POSITIVE SCHOOL MORALE FOR ALL

Anyone near the educational process for any length
of time realizes it is effective people, not complicated
programs, systems, or attractive teaching materials that
make the difference in learning for the students.
Positive, success-oriented teachers and administrators
can contribute to, and even create, an atmosphere of high-
level school morale for all concerned. Good morale means
feeling good about what we do as teachers, the setting
in which we do it, and the people with whom we associate
as we do our work. These feelings are greatly dependent
upon the degree of acceptance, love, and support that
we give and receive from significant other individuals.
When we feel cared for, are greeted warmly, have fellow
workers who listen to us, and have positive relationships
with students and parents, school is a good place. These
qualities create a sense of community and team spirit
in which it is much easier to carry out teaching and
learning.

Today, more than ever, there is a need for schools
to present an atmosphere where teachers can genuinely
make statements such as: "I am trusted and respected
as a person; I trust others with whom I teach; I am liked
and respected here; my efforts are appreciated by others;
I have input into school decisions." When this climate
exists for faculty, it is predictable that we will see
intellectual, emotional, and social growth in the

students. When we have succeeded in establishing such
a humane atmosphere or morale in our schools, it will
have been well worth the effort.

A FINAL WORD
     No longer should teachers feel they are short-
changing subject matter when they incorporate into their
teaching activities that involve attitudes and feelings
of self-worth, interpersonal communication, and values.
These humanistic activities help young people approach
self-knowledge, perhaps the most significant goal of
education. Traditional teaching styles, where the focus
is predominantly on subject matter, are inadequate for
educating young people in the life-coping skills necessary
to function fully in our present society. A definitive
need exists for learning how to relate to others, how
to be responsible, how to make decisions, and how to love.

REFERENCES AND SUGGESTED READINGS
Bloom, Benjamin. Human Characteristics and School
     Learning. New York: McGraw-Hill, 1976.
Bosher, Walton, C., and Albrecht, Karl G. Understanding
     People: Models and Concepts. San Diego, Calif.:
     University Associates, 1977.
Bradford, Leland P. Human Forces in Teaching and
     Learning. San Diego, Calif.: University
     Associates, 1976.
Brown, George Isaac. Human Teaching for Human Learning.
     New York: Viking, 1972.
Castillo, Gloria A. Left-Handed Teaching: Lessons in
     Affective Education. New York: Praeger, 1974.
Chazan, Barry I., and Soltis, Jonas F. Moral Education.
     New York: Teachers College Press, 1973.
Close, K. "Selecting Priorities at the White House
     Conference on Children." Children. 18(1)(1971):
     42-48.
Collins, Myrtle T., and Collins, Dwane R. Survival Kit
     for Teachers (and Parents). Santa Monica, Calif.:
     Goodyear, 1975.
Cromwell, Chester R., et al. Becoming: A Course in
     Human Relations Relating. New York: Lippincott,
     1975.
Ganley, Dr. Arnold L., and Elias, Dr. George S. Know
     Yourself. New York: McGraw-Hill, 1966.

Gazda, George M., et al. _Human Relations Development_.
    Boston: Allyn and Bacon, 1977.
Glasser, William. _The Identity Society_. New York:
    Harper & Row, 1972.
Hawley, Robert C., and Hawley, Isabel L. _Human Values
    in the Classroom_. New York: Hart, 1975.
James, Muriel, and Jongeword, Dorothy. _Born to Win:
    Transactional Analysis with Gestalt Experiments_.
    Reading, Mass.: Addison-Wesley, 1971.
Lippitt, Gordon, and Lippitt, Ronald. _The Consulting
    Process in Action_. San Diego, Calif.: University
    Associates, 1978.
Napier, Rodney W., and Gershenfeld, Matti K. _Groups:
    Theory and Experience_. Boston: Houghton Mifflin,
    1973.
Raths, Louis E. _Teaching for Learning_. Columbus,
    Ohio: Merrill, 1969.
Robert, Marc. _School Morale_. Niles, Ill.: Argus
    Communications, 1976.
Rogers, Carl R. _Carl Rogers on Encounter Groups_. New
    York: Harper & Row, 1970.
Rogers, Carl R. _Freedom to Learn_. Columbus, Ohio:
    Merrill, 1969.
Simon, Sidney B.; Howe, Leland W.; Kirschenbaum, Howard.
    Values Clarification. New York: Hart, 1972.
Tillich, Paul. _The Courage to Be_. New Haven and
    London: Yale University Press, 1971.
Tosi, Donald J. _Youth: Toward Personal Growth_.
    Columbus, Ohio: Merrill, 1974.

4

MULTICULTURAL EDUCATION: ITS ESSENCE AND CHALLENGE

Leander Brown

The impact of society upon education is so direct and constant that educators continually are discovering that the former beliefs about education's true course were based on an illusory glimpse. Educational philosophy, educational theory, and educational psychology have been in purposeful and continual evolution since the introduction of mid-eighteenth century Rousseauean thought. Thus, the pendulum of educational emphases has remained in constant motion. Classicism versus scientism, memory learning versus learning based upon firsthand knowledge, spiritually based education versus materially based education, have been but a few of the emphases propelling the pendulum from one extreme to the other.

Consistent with this established pattern, the latter half of the twentieth century also has been characterized by change, change occurring with such rapidity that educators have found themselves almost totally absorbed in a continuous grappling with the shifts in educational philosophy, educational theory, and educational psychology. Many of the shifts have, within the short span of a decade, flourished and then faded into obscurity. Most have tended to influence the movement of the pendulum by reversing its direction so that the ideological distance between emphases has continued to remain wide. The current back to basics thrust is not likely to shorten the arc.

The effects of these shifts upon educators have been varied and resist easy categorization. Yet, if you listen carefully to what many educators and researchers are saying, it becomes apparent that the frequent shifts in emphases have generated considerable cynicism, hostility,

and resistance. Moreover, the current emphases differ
from past emphases in that they make an impact upon the
teacher's personal values, beliefs, and background
experiences. Increasingly, such personal attributes are
being viewed as essential components of the educational
environment. In this regard, it seems to me that the
influence of the 1960s upon education is still being
felt. The push for freedom on the part of black Americans
has resulted in a like push for freedom on the part of
many subgroups within our society. Quality education,
whatever this term may mean, has been a central theme
in that push. Such innovations as team teaching, multiage
grouping, modular scheduling, open classrooms,
compensatory education, self-guided instruction, and
mainstreaming have been tried and are being tried in the
ongoing effort to achieve quality. The most significant
and distinctive characteristic of multicultural education
is that its designed effect is intended to modify the
educational experience for students in such a way that
educational quality is achieved for all. In a real sense
the only education deserving of the tremendous resources
poured into it by this society is multicultural
education. Whether practiced in the past or not, this
has always been true; and the extent to which we have
not had multicultural education is the extent to which
we have been shortchanged, or, more likely, miseducated.
    It can also be said that in a proper national
perspective of quality education, multicultural education
is a redundancy. That is to say, any education offered
as general education within a pluralistic society should,
by definition, be multicultural. The only alternative
would exist because oppression made it possible to exist.
This conclusion should raise some interesting questions
for educators and researchers as they ponder their past
and present roles in education. Still, to the credit
of the profession, some early educators within the United
States were sensitive and responsive to the dynamics of
multiculturalism, and were in fact in the forefront of
the push toward multicultural education. On the other
hand, it is probably to the discredit of the profession
that in some areas of the country state legislatures have
found it necessary to mandate multicultural education
standards for educators.

THE ESSENCE
    Simply put, "multicultural education is education

that values cultural pluralism." The term <u>multicultural</u> <u>education</u> becomes more meaningful when used as a term that describes a society or a nation. In the United States, a number of cultural groups and subgroups exist. Some of the differences that distinguish these groups are based upon identities associated with race, ethnicity, language, nationality, and religion.

It follows, then, that the term multicultural education should be attached to the education that is careful to provide a balanced perspective of society, including the positive, neutral, and sometimes negative contributions that the various groups and subgroups have made. It is important for us to stress that multicultural education is not contrived education; the balance sought is not to be artificial. While it is not realistic to assert that every group or subgroup has participated equally in every aspect of the society, it is certainly realistic to assert that all groups have participated and contributed in unique and various ways to the society.

I have found most education to be shaped to a greater or lesser degree by an ideological or philosophical premise of one sort or another. For example, in the United States and most western societies, a prevalent ideological orientation is that humankind is basically good. Consequently, multicultural education shaped by such a premise would, on balance, foster an understanding and an appreciation of each group and subgroup within the society consistent with that ideology.

Omissions, or a purely negative representation, of a group's or subgroup's contribution to society violates the concept of multicultural education. In a larger sense, it also violates the underlying ideological premise upon which education may be said to rest. The past absence of a multicultural emphasis in education, while pursuing the perhaps naive goal of assimilation, can be said to be vaguely credible. But what is less credible is the total disregard of a basic premise upon which public education has been held to rest. Had this premise been followed, it might well have helped to avoid some of the mistakes of the past, including that of thoughtlessly pursuing the goal of assimilation.

Because multicultural education fosters an understanding and an appreciation of the contributions of all the diverse groups within our society, it is an appropriate and important education for all members of society. The fact that a given population may be homogeneous in its makeup in no way diminishes this

point. It signifies, if anything, that the need for a
multicultural education would be even more critically
important than it might otherwise be for a more
heterogeneous population. The reasons for this should
be obvious.

Even if the foregoing proposition were totally
accepted, the successful delivery of multicultural
education will constitute a formidable challenge for
educators within the United States for perhaps the
remainder of this century. Multicultural curricula
materials are only in their infancy, and teachers will
need to bring extraordinary insights to bear as they
attempt to use existing materials from the past and
present in a multicultural context. Since today's
educators, for the most part, have not themselves been
exposed to such an education nor, for that matter, been
trained to deliver it, they will be severely handicapped
in this effort. Teacher education will have to retool,
a process in which it currently appears to be saying many
of the right things but is yet doing very little.

Another point to be cognizant about with regard to
curriculum is that multicultural education focuses upon
the contribution of groups and subgroups within a society
(multiethnic) as well as the contributions of those groups
without the society (multinational). The multiethnic
focus of multicultural education has been the most ignored
in the past. By this I mean a study of various countries
and continents, such as Africa, Asia, South America, or
Japan, is an appropriate study but it does not suffice
as the sum total of multicultural education.   A
multicultural focus within the United States would
necessarily include the contributions of such groups as
Afro-Americans, Native Americans, Japanese Americans,
etc. As James A. Banks describes it, the multiethnic
and multinational focuses both are aspects of a
multicultural education.

MULTICULTURAL CURRICULUM--WHERE TO BEGIN

Because multicultural education is such a wide-
ranging concept, its implications can pose problems for
educators who prefer curricula with clean entry and exit
points. The great number of ethnic groups within the
United States militates against accomplishing such
curricula objectives. Still, in most such instances,
an appropriate initial emphasis should be multiethnic

in nature. This suggestion generally elicits the
observation that such an undertaking can be extremely
unwieldy and likely to yield doubtful results,
particularly if a teacher endeavors to include all
existing ethnic groups in the curriculum. Yet a
multiethnic focus does not mandate that all ethnic groups
must be focused upon.

A multicultural education curriculum ideal for one
locality will not necessarily be ideal for another.
Typically, the ethnic groups included in such a curriculum
consist of those groups within the society known to have
suffered from such discriminations: Native Americans,
Appalachian Americans, Afro-Americans, and Mexican
Americans, as well as the ethnic groups represented in
the locality itself. The primary objective here is to
foster a better understanding and appreciation of self
as well as of others and, having acquired this
perspective, to positively influence the relationships
among ethnically different persons.

THE CHALLENGE

Given the nature of the dominant American lifestyle
for the past two centuries, the successful delivery of
a multiethnic education for the educator will be much
like traversing a minefield that is threatening to explode
into an all-consuming atmosphere of alienation between
ethnically different educators and students.
Unfortunately, so many potentially disruptive social mines
have been laid that it is impossible to alert teachers
to all of them. Thus, teachers are left in many respects
to traverse this course using only their instincts.

Teachers are capable of minimizing the hazards of
the journey, however, by taking care to avoid at least
those mines that populate the field to a higher proportion
than others: those where value judgments are used
inappropriately, where patronization is practiced, or
where victim analysis is performed. All these have the
effect of communicating lack of respect and dignity for
the person or group concerned.

The multiethnic education mines mentioned here are
attitudinal and strategic in character. They differ
primarily in the degree to which they are conscious or
unconscious attempts of teachers to manipulate students
or students' ideas. The observable characteristics of
the value judgment mine suggest that it is often more

unconscious and attitudinal in nature rather than strategic. On the other hand, patronization and victim analysis seem to be more the result of conscious strategizing. Both kinds of mines, nevertheless, are of the genre that educators ought be most concerned with.

Value Judgment Mine

A value judgment mine that many educators fail to avoid is the discounting of the values brought into the educational environment by the ethnically different student. The usual outcome is that almost always the student is forced to experience discomfort and alienation. Another variation of the value judgment mine is that the educator simply imposes upon the student the educator's values, which of course are presumed to be correct. This action often achieves the identical result as does the discounting action unless due care is exercised.

The above examples are but two examples of value judgment mines. There are countless others, and unless we understand how values influence our lives we are destined to trip over them. Another valid reason for studying the valuing process is that schools are, by their nature, value repositories. If they were not there would be no need to be concerned with multiculturalism.

The process of urging students to clarify their values is an essential part of a quality education but, in addition, educators from time to time may find they need to subject students to imposed values. This seemingly should not require an apology on the part of the educator because the process is after all a universal teaching strategy used not only by educators but by parents and other care-givers as well. However, a strong caveat should be observed when such a process is used. Mainly, that due care is exercised--that the teacher is absolutely cognizant of what values are being imposed and what ethically defensible rationale, consistent with the basic principles of education, compels it.

Patronization Mine

The strategic multiethnic mines owe some of their explosive potency not only to the educator's attitudes, but also to a possible lack of awareness and sensitivity. In this regard, I previously mentioned patronization. Patronization is a practice that careless educators are engaged in when they are not genuinely interested in multiethnic education, but for one reason or another feel compelled to do something for the sake of appearance.

Many strategies are born out of this motivation. A typical example is the taking of an ethnic experience from one context and using it in a context unrelated to any perceived academic or artistic purpose that gives it true educational significance. Obviously, if this is the educator's motivation, it would be better if ethnic experiences were left in the ethnic community. For until an educator has acquired the insight and understanding necessary for using that experience in an educationally meaningful and positive way, it is improper to use it. Doing otherwise is more likely to encourage cynicism on the part of students more than to accomplish anything positive; students will recognize the educator's efforts as a ploy even if he or she fails to recognize it as such.

The patronization mine can be avoided by simply ensuring that the ethnic materials or experiences used in the classroom contribute to an understanding and appreciation of the ethnic group's relationship to the students. Admittedly, for many, this kind of pedagogical expertise is not acquired easily. It will require serious thought, study, patience, and a positive attitude.

Victim Analysis Mine

The etiology for the mines of victim analysis is much the same as that for the mines of patronization. The manifestation of this approach is embodied in the process whereby the educator identifies an ethnic group and proceeds to amplify upon its values, traditions, customs, virtues, and, almost assuredly, its pathologies as if the group was an isolate within the society. The social issues having impact upon that ethnic group will be viewed to exist solely as a result of the actions or inactions of that particular group. Victim analysis is operative also when the educator seeks to bring in any available ethnic person for a personal interview. There is nothing inherently wrong, of course, in bringing ethnic experiences into the classroom; after all, it is a valid multiethnic experience. What is wrong, however, is to introduce that experience into the classroom in a way that does injustice to the multiethnic group by creating and reinforcing stereotypes that become barriers to understanding and to forming positive relationships.

MORE ABOUT STRATEGIES AND ATTITUDES

In the past two decades many educators have been busy devising and categorizing strategies and techniques

for working with a multicultural student body. These
efforts have been both individual and collective, and
include both multiethnic and multinational ideas for
curricula. Indeed, many school systems around the country
have formed task forces to produce multicultural
curricula.

At present, the limits on the ability to deliver
a multicultural education rests more in the pedagogical
skills of teachers than in the materials and strategies
available to them. Recognizing that this limitation
constitutes a serious impediment to the delivery of a
multicultural education, many school districts have
devised inservice programs in an attempt to update such
teaching skills. State departments of instruction are
encouraging or requiring the acquisition of course work
in the area of multicultural education for the issuance
or renewal of teaching certificates.

Unfortunately, these pressures in some instances
have had the effect of channeling educators into inservice
with facilitators who hold dubious credentials for this
extremely difficult and sensitive assignment. In spite
of this, some positive results can be claimed. Whether
they can be said to have occurred because of the inservice
or in spite of it is a question that could consume
considerable time and discussion. At the same time,
however, we must come to grips also with the disturbing
realization that the number of educators emerging from
these inservice efforts with cynicism, hostility, and,
in some cases, almost a commitment to the active sabotage
of multicultural education programs is too large to be
satisfied that success has been achieved. Obviously,
the quality of the inservices has been varied. Some
states have achieved a conspicuous excellence in their
multicultural efforts. California and Minnesota are two
notable examples and I would like to believe that Iowa
is improving.

Teachers should be ever-mindful that one of the
primary difficulties in the delivery of a multicultural
education rests in the fact that the effort involves not
only the cognitive quality of what is offered the student,
but also the affective quality embodied within the teacher
who offers it. In other words, educators should be what
Carl Rogers calls "congruent." Teachers deal often with
value-laden content. Therefore, the successful
communication of that content will be enhanced if they
show, through behaviors and interactions, that they
believe value differences and cultural diversities are

life-enriching experiences. Teachers can begin this process by showing an appreciation for the unique values and diversity present within the classroom itself.

A good reason for establishing an appreciation of value and cultural differences within the classroom may be apparent from the following example. In most schools within our society some attempt is made to recognize black history for a week or a month. Teachers will no doubt be asked why this is important. The question can be a perfectly reasonable one if the questioner has no appreciation for his or her own uniqueness or his or her relationship to historical antecedents. The educator cannot assume that this process has already taken place. This is why the classroom must be established as a multicultural microcosm.

Thus, multicultural education can be both simple and complex at the same time. A failure to appreciate this fact can even be seen in the actions of experienced educators and administrators. Earlier, I alluded to the fact that inservices in multicultural education required enormous skill, patience, and insight on the part of the facilitator in order to effect change and improvement in affective qualities. Yet, educators and administrators have been known to assign facilitative responsibilities to persons on the basis of their being a "good person" or on the basis of their being identified as a member of a given ethnic or minority group, regardless of any other qualifications.

This practice is cited to emphasize the point that understanding or commitment to multicultural education is not overabundant. Therefore, educators' growth in this area beyond a superficial level may not come easily. Perhaps they should feel that if such achievement does come easily they ought to be suspicious.

The factor of racism and its undermining effect upon achieving multicultural education is another problem that must be met head-on. Usually, the intellectual and emotional blockage that accompanies this issue constitutes the greatest barrier to attitudinal change on the part of the educator. Educators are reluctant to concede that, like nearly everyone else in United States society, they are likely to be racist and sexist. Racism, in this context, means racism as defined by Robert W. Terry:

> Racism exists when one race/color group intentionally refuses to share power, distributes resources inequitably, maintains unresponsive and

inflexible institutional policies, procedures and
practices, and imposes ethnocentric culture on any
race/color group for its supposed benefit, and
justifies its actions by blaming the other race/color
group.

Terry's definition for sexism is almost a parallel to
the above definition of racism except that the word
sexism replaces racism and the words gendercentric
and gender replace ethnocentric and race/color.
     It should not be hard to understand the elusiveness
of conveying this concept, or in understanding the
resistance to it, when it is noted that even inservice
facilitators can be observed communicating the dictum
that we are racist while at the same time they are unaware
of the fact that it describes themselves as well. Indeed,
it would seem most imperative at this juncture that the
facilitator be a knowledgeable, skillful, and positive
model of the attitudes and behaviors that he or she is
trying to teach. This is important and critical because
under the best of circumstances, educators confronted
with this proposition find it extremely difficult and
painful to accept. Still, it is difficult to understand
how anyone could be reared in this society and come to
believe otherwise.
     Even after arriving at this point of acknowledged
prejudice it is extremely important that further self-
understanding be developed. For the aspiring
multicultural educator, this consciousness-raising can
be, and usually is, a significant beginning point because
it creates an awareness level from which one can move
toward better interpersonal relationships. It may help
if educators regard it as similar to the treatment so
effective with alcoholics. That is to say, improvement
is not possible until the problem is acknowledged.
     Imagine the potential impact on ethnically different
school children in particular, and all students in
general, if teachers awoke each morning and resolved,
"Today I will strive hard not to be racist or sexist."
Because we live in a highly pluralistic society, teachers
must continually make some such commitment or they are
almost destined to be racist or sexist to one degree or
another.
     Because the mines in the field to be traversed in
the delivery of a multicultural education are so subtle
and diverse, arriving at this life position will not

eliminate the possibility that mishaps will occur. They will occur, but they should be fewer and they should be less likely to be mines that will explode into catastrophic hostility and alienation. Many effective teachers are already making great strides to deliver a quality education to all children.

REFERENCES AND SUGGESTED READINGS
American Association of Colleges for Teacher Education Commission on Multicultural Education. "No One Model American." Journal of Teacher Education 24 (Winter 1973): 264-65.
Banks, James A. "The Implications of Multicultural Education for Teacher Education." Pluralism and the American Teacher: Issues and Case Studies. Frank H. Klassen, and Donna M. Gollnick, eds. Washington, D.C.: Ethnic Heritage Center for Teacher Education, American Association of Colleges for Teacher Education, 1977.
Grant, Carl A. Multicultural Education: Committments, Issues and Applications. Washington, D.C.: Association for Supervision and Curriculum Development, Multicultural Education Commission, 1977.
Hunter, William A. Multicultural Education through Competency-Based Teacher Education. Washington, D.C.: Association of Colleges for Teacher Education, 1974.
Rogers, Carl R. On Becoming a Person. Boston: Houghton Mifflin, 1961.
Suzuki, Bob H. "Multicultural Education: What's It All About?" Integrated Education 17 (1979): 43-50.
Terry, Robert W. For Whites Only. Rev. ed. Grand Rapids, Mich.: Eerdmans, 1977.

5

THE THINGS
SUCCESSFUL TEACHERS DO

James E. Albrecht.

Secondary school principals probably do more teacher evaluation than anyone else in the educational system. This chapter is a discussion of the techniques commonly employed by the teachers I have judged to be the most effective over the past twenty-six years.

During the course of those evaluations, I came gradually to recognize that, to an almost astonishing degree, teachers I judged to be effective consistently did certain quite specific things in a manner very different from the way those same things were handled by teachers I judged to be ineffective.

It is incorrect to assume that every effective teacher performs every one of these actions at an ideal level. It is also incorrect to assume that every ineffective teacher is an abject failure in each of those areas. I am convinced, however, that effective teachers do most of these things well. I am also convinced that ineffective teachers have serious deficiencies in at least some of these areas.

CLASSROOM ACTIVITIES AND MATERIALS

Master teachers, like good airline pilots, have a clear sense of their destination. They know, each time they step into a classroom, where they are going and that the destination must be defined in terms of what happens to students as a result of the classroom experience.

An effective teacher thinks about what students should <u>know</u>, or be able to <u>do</u>, or how they should <u>feel</u> about something as a result of the classroom experience the teacher has prepared. In some instances, a combination of these outcomes may be appropriate to the classroom experience, but the teacher must have a clear sense of what should happen to students at the completion of each instructional session. A distinctive characteristic of the work of effective teachers is that the activities and learning materials in his or her classroom are clearly appropriate to the outcomes sought from the instruction. Simply put, the things the students are doing and the materials they're working with are closely suited to what the teacher wants those students to know, or feel, or be able to do by the close of the session.

Once the effective teacher has made that determination, the stage is set for the next key decision the teacher must make. The sense of destination is critical, but the next decision is one of means. How do we get students to that destination? What methods and materials are suited to the ends we've identified? What do we want students to study, and how do we want them to study it?

Ineffective teachers are often insensitive to the fact that how a youngster is studying something may be more important than what specific material is being studied, particularly if the outcome sought centers on the student's ability to do something, or to develop a sensitivity to or feeling about something.

Effective teachers know that some ends of instruction are best served by scrupulous attention to content while other ends of instruction are best served by attention to process.

Even when the purpose of instruction focuses on the students' knowing something they didn't know before, good teachers understand that no one "owns" a piece of knowledge until that person can make that knowledge work for him or her, can use it and apply it. So the good teacher creates activities that permit the students to apply their knowledge and eventually to feel they "own" it.

ROLES FOR LEARNERS

Skilled teachers involve students in the deliberations and activities of the classroom. Many secondary teachers apparently assume such involvement is primarily appropriate to the elementary classroom and has little to do with secondary education. They are wrong. Learners at all levels must have a sense that they're actively engaged with the subject matter. The younger the student, the truer that is.

The challenge for the secondary teacher is much greater in some academic areas than in others. The typing teacher, the home economics teacher, the physical education teacher, and the art teacher all have ready-made opportunities for students to grapple actively with the major dimensions of the subject matter. Astute teachers in science and mathematics are able to seize the problem-solving opportunities that can thrust students into active problem-solver roles.

The teacher in language arts and social studies, however, faces a more troublesome situation. The disciplines themselves do not automatically suggest a role for learners that forces them to engage the subject in an active way. Consequently, it is not unusual to see students in those classes spending a disproportionate amount of their time listening. And they are nearly always (supposed to be) listening to their teacher, who assumes that if they have listened carefully and--most sacred of all--taken notes, they will be rewarded by achieving a high grade on "the test."

While there is something to be said for note taking and effective listening, they hardly qualify as the characteristics most often cited by students who believe they have had an opportunity to engage their subject. Students in most subjects must be given chances to confront conjecture and dilemma and to try out ideas on one another as well as on the teacher. They need to have the opportunity to play roles, to draw conclusions from primary source material, to prowl through the intricacies of institutions and regulations so they may discern for themselves the common characteristics and big ideas that make things work, and do the hundreds of other things that cause students to believe they have been active participants in their own learning.

Students will be active, sooner or later, in the classroom; the skilled teacher finds opportunities to channel that need for active involvement into areas where it can be an important asset to the learning environment. The unskilled teacher too often provides no appropriate and useful outlet for it, then spends days of frustration wondering why students will not accept happily the passive roles in which they have been cast by the teacher.

GIVING OF ASSIGNMENTS

Teachers often tend to give hurried and incomplete assignments; even good teachers suffer lapses here. Too many times assignments are given to students when, for all practical purposes, the instructional period is already over. The assignment, therefore, becomes something to be dispatched as quickly as possible in the fewest words possible. "For tomorrow, read Chapter 24." That's far too typical and far too unproductive.

Master teachers recognize the importance of giving an assignment carefully. After all, that assignment's probably going to be the foundation of the next day's work. Sufficient time needs to be reserved to make certain the assignment receives the attention it deserves; it can't be done as an afterthought when the period ends.

A characteristic of an adequate assignment is that the student's accountability for the assignment is specified. If, for instance, the chapter contains two or three key points students must know, those points should be discussed briefly in advance and the students' responsibility for them established. (If parts of the chapter are relatively unimportant, in terms of the teacher's goal for the unit, there's nothing wrong in the teacher's saying that to the students and suggesting that those parts be skimmed or even ignored.)

Good teachers also help students understand the reading approach they should use in studying the assigned material. If parts of the assignment require careful study for details, that should be made clear when the teacher gives the assignment. If a large segment of the assignment needs first to be read quickly so that a critical perspective may be gained by the student, then reread with care to see how the components relate to that perspective, that should be indicated by the teacher. The correct reading approach to understanding the assignment materials may be instinctively understood by bright students who read well, but for many other students the teacher's assistance is essential.

Difficulties in the assignment should also be identified by the teacher. Vocabulary deficiencies are prevalent enough in most classes to justify a singling out of specialized or infrequently used words when giving the assignment. A typical student who comes across the word <u>ubiquitous</u> in the first paragraph of a lengthy

reading assignment is quite likely to close the book on
the spot with a resigned sigh (or a mild expletive),
assuming he or she is simply hopelessly outmatched. If
the teacher, however, has told that student that the word
will be confronted early in the assignment and that it
means "present everywhere," the typical student is far
more likely to feel up to the challenge of completing
the assignment when the word is encountered. The teacher
has given the student at least some of the key
understandings required for success in handling some of
the obstacles the assigned reading contains.

Effective teachers are equally attentive in assigning
written work. Again, assigning written work requires
a substantial amount of time if the assignment is given
with the sort of care it merits. Students shouldn't have
to ask the questions that typically abound in classrooms
where assignments are hastily or carelessly given. "How
long does it have to be? Should we use pen or pencil?
May we write on both sides of the paper? May we outline,
or do we have to use complete sentences? Will you count
off for spelling mistakes?" And on and on.

Of course, such questions need not arise because
the teacher should have explained that--and much more.
The important features of the assignment should be
identified and discussed, and the special qualities of
the student's work that will be rewarded and penalized
should be clearly understood by the students after the
assignment is given.

Teachers should do what they reasonably can to strip
away the uncertainties and the inconsequentials of the
assignment, thus enabling students to focus on the
important elements of the assignment.

The master teacher works hard to present assignments
in a way that encourages students to feel they know
precisely what's expected of them and how they should
proceed to meet that expectation. Students simply should
not have to guess about assignments.

ESTABLISHING THE RATIONALE
New teachers are often disconcerted by the
persistence of some contentious students who demand to
know why certain assignments are given, why certain
activities are required, and why certain topics are
studied by the class. If the teacher has not thought

through the why of such matters ahead of time, answering such questions may reveal clearly that the rationale is, in fact, shaky or confused. His or her uncertainty exacerbates the situation and is a guarantee that nearly everything the teacher asks the class to do in the immediate future will be promptly followed by more such questions. If the teacher refuses to answer such questions, the resultant hostility becomes a permanent characteristic of the classroom.

The effect of all this is to create, sometimes in a subtle and almost unnoticed fashion, a climate in the classroom that is adversarial in nature--the teacher on one side, the students on the other. Inevitably, rapport between teacher and students suffers dramatically as a consequence.

Good teachers avoid that sitation through the simple act of preempting the "why do we have to" questions. As topics are selected for study, as assignments are given, and as activities are prescribed, the effective teacher accompanies the directions with an explanation of why the class is being asked to do whatever it is that's being required. While not all students will accept all explanations for all activities, the fact that the explanation is offered at the teacher's initiative is of tremendous psychological importance.

Explanations can also address the drudgery an assignment entails--for example, learning the parts of irregular verbs and memorizing the names associated with place geography. On these occasions, the teachers can explain why such knowledge is important, then tell the students how miserable they will be in doing the work. The teacher can call it, "boring, dull, routine, monotonous, dollar-a-day work."

Interestingly, in a curious manifestation of reverse psychology, the students react as though intrigued by the challenge. They approach the work with enthusiasm, as if to prove they cannot be discouraged by such a pessimistic characterization of the work required of them.

The important element is the initiative taken by the teacher in explaining to the students the value and importance of what they're doing. If such explanations appear to be dragged from a teacher reluctant (or unable) to give them, then the students sense a subtle shift in the teacher-student relationship in the classroom. When that happens, the classroom environment presents a formidable obstacle to effective teaching and learning. Good teachers don't let that happen.

THE CLASSROOM ATMOSPHERE

Some teachers have difficulty creating a classroom environment clearly suited to the demands of effective learning. Part of the reason, at least for some teachers, is their inability to identify in their own minds the elements that characterize the ideal learning environment.

I am convinced that all classrooms that present ideal learning environments are <u>pleasant</u>, <u>relaxed</u>, and <u>efficient</u>. Those three qualities mark the ideal atmosphere in which youngsters learn best.

Unfortunately, some teachers concentrate their efforts on one or two--but not all--of these qualities. When carried to extremes an unbalanced, exclusive emphasis on efficiency can create a classroom atmosphere reminiscent of Ossining's Maximum Security Wing. On the other hand, the same sort of exclusive emphasis on the pleasant relaxed dimensions can create an atmosphere that resembles Mardi Gras. The trick, of course, is to keep all three qualities in healthy balance.

Students learn best when they are relaxed and free from artificial tension; when the relationship among students and between students and teacher is pleasant; and when the efforts of both the teacher and students are centered on an efficient, businesslike approach to the subject under study.

The characteristics identified earlier in this chapter are directly related to producing precisely that sort of learning environment, but it is important that teachers know what the characteristics are so they may consciously work to cultivate them in their classrooms.

In addition to the suggestions already given, good teachers also enhance the learning environment by trying to praise students publicly while criticizing them privately. The impact of that effort upon the classroom atmosphere is significant. While it is not always possible to manage that, effective teachers make a constant effort to do so.

CLASSROOM QUESTIONS

In most classrooms questions abound. Many are asked by the teacher, many by students. The manner in which these questions are handled has a great deal to do with maintaining a desirable classroom environment, as well as providing students insights into the subject being studied.

Unfortunately, not all questions asked by students

are probing, thoughtful attempts to reach more sophisticated understanding of the subject. Some are, in fact, apparently unrelated in any way to that goal. They are, in short, bothersome, irrelevant, and unwelcome intrusions into the flow of intellectual discourse.

Teachers are often understandably irritated by such questions, and many of them exhibit that irritation in obvious ways. Often teachers dismiss such questions as "stupid," or suggest that the question "makes no sense." Frequently they are correct in that characterization. However, if one accepts the notion that student questions should be handled from the premise that they are sincerely motivated--and they usually are--then the good teacher does not succumb to that irritation. Instead, the teacher remembers that students (and their questions) should be treated with courtesy and respect, since that approach is the best guarantee that those qualities will in turn be extended to the teacher by the students. If that classroom modeling is shattered because the teacher becomes irritated, the possible implications for teacher-student relationships are unpleasant.

The ploy often used by effective teachers in this situation is to say, "That's an interesting question, but I don't think this is the best moment to pursue it. Let me set it on a shelf for a bit [or hang it on a hook] and we'll come back to it."

The student now feels that the question had merit. In fact, it is going to receive "special" attention, and the student feels good about that. Yet the class is not diverted at an untimely moment from desired closure.

An interesting side effect is that often other students note that questions a little out of the ordinary do get considered. Consequently, a subtle encouragement for divergent thinking in the classroom begins to emerge, and students often begin to think creatively about the application of the basic ideas and the concepts under discussion. And that, of course, is all to the good.

When teachers pose the questions, a different group of considerations arise. I have noted three common mistakes teachers make in their classroom questioning. The first is illustrated by this question actually posed by an instructor who told me his instructional goal was to "get his students to think." At the very start of the period he asked, "How about the Depression?" The class members were absolutely blank, looking over their shoulders and sideways to try to pick up a clue from other students. One could almost hear them thinking, "What does he want to know? When did it occur? What was its impact? What were its characteristics? What precipitated it?"

The teacher, angry at the lack of response, reacted angrily to the class. But the fault lay with the question. It was a poor question, indeed a stupid question, because it was imprecise. Students really did not know what was being asked of them.

Unfortunately that sort of question is asked all too often by teachers, and the deficiency is always the same, that is, students do not know what the teacher wants from them in response to the question because the question lacks clarity and precision.

A second common failing in teacher-initiated questions is to begin a question by saying, "Charlie, . . ." which has the immediate effect, for some students, of excusing them from the deliberations. In that situation, many students not named Charlie take a vacation from deep thought because they assume Charlie will take care of things.

Sometimes, of course, Charlie doesn't take care of the question; he doesn't know the answer. The teacher then turns to another student, sometimes to one of those on a self-declared vacation, and is dismayed to find that the student not only doesn't know the answer, he or she doesn't even know the question.

Again the fault lies, at least in part, with the way the question is asked. If the teacher delays identifying the respondent until after all questions are posed, the attention of all the class will be engaged on the question, simply because each class member will have been aware that he or she might well become the identified respondent. That partially insures that the question will at least register and perhaps receive some contemplation by most members of the class. Though the procedure does not guarantee that everyone will know the answer, it does substantially improve the likelihood that everyone will at least know the question.

The third common and troublesome practice apparent in the questions teachers ask is posing several questions all at once. I once observed an English teacher who began a class by asking, "How many of you have read Lord of the Flies? Or how many of you saw the movie? And which

one did you like best?" Perhaps three seconds separated
the three questions; thus, for the class, the separate
questions had the appearance of one.

The reaction of the class was predictable. Confusion
reigned. Several students confidently raised their hands
to indicate they'd read the book, but when asked
immediately about the film, many hesitantly put down their
hands while others tentatively raised theirs. When the
third part of the question was posed, everyone resignedly
dropped their hands. The question was simply too much.

It wasn't in reality a single question at all; it
was a series of questions masquerading as one. Again,
students were frustrated and irritated because the way
the question(s) was posed in effect took from them their
opportunity for involvement and denied them an opportunity
for recognition of their achievement.

Effective teachers are continually aware of these
potential pitfalls and phrase questions carefully to avoid
them. Master teachers know that one of the purposes of
their questions is to eliminate student confusion and
uncertainty, not to add to them.

EXAMPLES AND ILLUSTRATIONS

If one asks students what they value in the teachers
they believe to be best, sooner or later reference is
made to the teacher's ability to "explain things so we
understand them." Such teachers use illustrations and
examples lavishly and effectively, and students obviously
respond to that.

Ineffective teachers often have difficulty helping
youngsters grasp complicated ideas. My observations
suggest that one of the reasons for that is the teacher's
preparation of only one explanation for a given idea.
When that explanation is exhausted and clarification is
still inadequate for some students, there's nothing left
for the teacher to turn to.

Skilled teachers, however, anticipate the possibility
of some student confusion for almost any idea. They arm
themselves with a variety of weaponry as they approach
even simple concepts, sure in the knowledge that if any
given weapon seems inadequate to clarify things, another
is available.

If a student says, "I don't get it," the skilled
teacher is able to say, "Well, let me give you another
example." That teacher understands the critical role

played by multiple illustrations and varied examples and
knows that while some students respond to broad
explanations others gain insights through instances of
specific application of abstract ideas or principles.

Skilled teachers also understand that any opportunity
that allows comparisons to be drawn between the topic
under study and phenomena in contemporary society is
particularly productive. Students who are led to
visualize the applicability and relevance of "academic"
notions to the time and place they inhabit are eventually
likely to understand the ideas being considered. Students
who seldom have those parallels pointed out for them may
never understand the notions or appreciate their
significance.

Creative teachers amuse themselves (and serve their
students well) by conjuring up a vast storehouse of
anecdotes, examples, and illustrations that may help to
clarify, at least for some students, the topics they plan
to pursue in the future. They are always sensitive to
developments in contemporary society that point up the
relevance of those topics, and they become skilled at
underscoring the critical elements common to those
contemporary developments and the topics.

It is not unusual for students to boast that they
are able to dredge up from their memories a complicated
idea simply by recalling an anecdote or a specific example
or application that was originally presented by one of
their teachers. Perhaps that, as much as anything,
provides hard evidence for the value of effective
illustrations of key ideas and basic concepts. They help
students to understand and, eventually, they help them
to learn.

CLASSROOM DISCUSSIONS

For many teachers the dominant classroom activity
is discussion. Certainly the activity, particularly in
some disciplines, is a valuable tool, accomplishing
certain ends of education perhaps better than any other.

In the hands of a skilled teacher, a classroom
discussion is normally a fascinating and vital
experience. Unfortunately, classroom discussions may
also be essentially a kind of intellectual milling about.
If so, there often is no purpose to all the interchange
or, if one is present, it is only dimly apparent to the
participants. The whole activity often apparently has

no direction, largely because the goal either is not identified or is not kept clearly in focus.

Almost every classroom, however, is equipped with a simple device that can be used by the teacher to improve the quality of classroom dicussions. The device is the chalkboard, or its more sophisticated equivalent, the overhead projector. Skilled utilization of either tool provides the summarizing and direction-giving dimension so often lacking in mediocre, or just plain inferior classroom discussion.

Since discussions range so widely in purpose, dependent partially upon the discipline in which they are employed, generalizing about correct procedure is not useful. The use of the chalkboard, however, often may include the following practices, all designed to give the summarizing and direction-giving dimensions mentioned above:

1. Identifying in writing the central purposes of the discussion, thus providing students a sense of what is intended to happen as an outgrowth of the activity.
2. Summarizing periodically in writing the progress made in the discussion, noting particularly the key points which have emerged--especially those that bear upon the previously identified purposes.
3. Identifying in writing those significant student observations that may open unanticipated aspects of the topic for future consideration, or those that provide perceptive insights into some facet of the topic.
4. Summarizing in writing at the close of the discussion the progress made toward the destination specified at the beginning of the activity.
5. Indicating in writing the relationship of what has been produced by the day's work to what remains to be done in future discussion, thus providing students perspective, a sense of how things fit together.

The stress on writing on the board is important. The carefully recorded purposes, summaries, significant observations, and future intent all are tangibly and visibly placed before the student at appropriate times during the discussion. This visible record is, in many ways, analogous to the map to which drivers and passengers often refer when in the process of making a sizeable trip.

The skilled teacher creates, through the use of the chalkboard or overhead projector, a similar sort of map for the class members who are accompanying him or her on a different sort of trip to a different sort of observation. Students given that sort of experience seldom respond, when asked what they did during the class period, "Oh, we just talked about a bunch of stuff." Instead, they generally know not only what was discussed, but to what end it was discussed.

MANAGING SMALL GROUPS

Another strategy often used by teachers is providing opportunities for students to interact with one another in small-group settings. Again, for some purposes of instruction this may be an extremely important approach, getting at certain types of outcomes which no other approach can match.

Small-group work is often, however, far less effective than it should be. There is a natural and understandable inclination for youngsters (and often adults, as well) to "waste" an inordinate amount of time in such settings. The problem is often exacerbated by teachers who fail to employ effective management techniques.

With the possible exception of classes made up of the most able and committed students, I am convinced that for small-group work teachers should employ quite rigid and direct approaches. Failure to do so generally creates confusion and an inefficient use of valuable time--too high a price to pay for any instructional technique.

Generally, good management technique for small-group work includes the following components:

1. Establishing the size of the group. The directive, "Break up into groups" usually results in clusters of two to eight students suddenly sprouting in the classroom. That won't do, of course, so the teacher is eventually forced either to live with that disparity or to identify the limits of group size--which should have been done anyway at the start of the activity.
2. Identifying specific students for inclusion in specific groups. This is important for two reasons. First, it provides the teacher with some control over the social chemistry of the group. This is especially

critical with younger students, many of whom make
choices governed almost completely by their own social
needs.

The result is that the composition of any given
group is exclusively social and those who are social
isolates in the class either must force their way
into a group where they are unwelcome or suffer the
indignity of being rejected by groups free to choose
their own membership.

If the isolated students are adroitly identified
by the teacher for inclusion in a specific group,
much of the anxiety and hurt feelings suffered by
these youngsters can be avoided.

The second reason for recommending that pupil
selection be left to the teacher is to provide balance
among the groups. If one group is dominated by
students at a concrete operational level, and another
dominated by students at a formal operational level,
overall group balance is destroyed. Ideally, groups
(at least for most educational purposes) should
contain a suitable and reasonable mix of leaders and
nonleaders, males and females, minority and majority
students, and able and less able students. That's
not likely to happen if the teacher doesn't see to
it.

3. Identifying key roles to be assumed by members of
   the group. If students are given the responsibility
   for selecting the group chair and group recorder,
   if the latter is required by the activity, some
   abstract principle of democracy or self-determination
   may be served. However, an undue amount of time will
   probably be consumed by the nomination and election
   process and, more significantly, some students will
   probably never receive an opportunity to serve in
   those positions. Teacher designation can take care
   of all that.

4. Establishing those specific responsibilities for
   which the entire group will be held accountable, and
   those for which the chair and the recorder will be
   held accountable. If group members are to receive
   the full benefits of group work, they need to
   recognize for what the group will be held
   responsible so they can evaluate individual
   contributions in light of an established, recognized
   goal.

If the group's efforts are to be rewarded or penalized in some formal manner, it makes good sense to give the group that information before it begins its deliberations. The responsibilities borne by the chair and recorder also require equal attention. Minutes, summaries, recommendations, conclusions-- whatever is expected of the group's officers--should be carefully delineated, as should any special considerations governing those obligations.

5. Suggesting mechanical guidelines. After students have become experienced in small-group processes, they may be able to work effectively with no suggestions related to mechanics. Until they've gained that experience, however, teachers need to recognize that suggesting procedures to aid the group in its deliberations; suggesting time deadlines for moving from one dimension of the problem to the next; and periodically listening in on the deliberations may be keys to the effectiveness with which the group members operate.

Often the difference between those classrooms in which small-group processes are useful and productive and those classrooms in which they are largely an ineffective waste of time is simply a matter of the teacher's skill in managing the small-group operation. If a teacher hopes to make the efficient use of instructional time an important consideration in the classroom, it is imperative that these key management initiatives be taken by the teacher in employing small-group activities.

SPECIAL TEACHER INITIATIVES

The preceding section contains a reference to the teacher's listening in on small-group discussions as a useful method of improving the quality of those discussions. That suggests an initiative that skilled teachers contantly seize, though they do not limit it to small-group work.

Really effective teachers are forever alert for the opportunity to do what we so often talk about in education and so seldom do, namely, work on the individual differences present in our classrooms.

When teachers typically are confronted everyday by five classes of twenty-seven or more students each, it

is hardly surprising that they seldom have the chance
to do much with individual students. Indeed the wonder
is that they do as well as they do.

Nevertheless, the need for special attention to
individual students does not go away, and the effective
teacher recognizes the constancy of that need. It is
largely when students are at work in the classroom on
individual or small-group assignments that the opportunity
for individual attention is available to any substantial
degree. And that's when the effective teacher seizes
the initiative.

It is clearly difficult, and often impolitic, to
single out students for special attention when that has
to be done within the hearing of the entire class. Yet,
for many students, it makes good sense to modify an
assignment, to make it either more or less demanding.
For other students it makes good sense to suggest an
alternative to the assigned source of information, perhaps
a film strip or a simple reading reference. Some students
may profit from having the teacher provide the opening
two sentences of a writing assignment, while others may
benefit from having an unusual writing approach required
of them. (I've known students who improved their writing
skills dramatically when a teacher required they write
no sentence longer than ten words when fulfilling an
assignment.) All these things are much easier to do if
the teacher takes the initiative to move among students
while they are engaged in what was once quaintly referred
to as "seat work."

A key to being an effective learning resource for
students is to be easily accessible to them while they
are working on assignments. That accessibility is, of
course, increased if the teacher is strolling among
students while they work, rather than relaxing behind
a desk.

As the teacher moves through the class, he or she
is in a good position to offer gentle corrections for
work already inaccurately or incorrectly in progress,
encouragement for the expansion of promising ideas being
developed by students or for unusual insights being
demonstrated, subtle nudges to the procrastinator, and
reinforcement for particularly valuable contributions
made by class members. (Students thrill to being told
privately and directly by the teacher, "Diane, I want
you to know how much I appreciate the quality of the work
you've been doing lately." That sort of encouragement

can affect a youngster's entire attitude toward a specific class, or even toward education generally.)

None of this can occur if a teacher retires to his or her desk while students work on assignments. To be sure, some of the more secure, more aggressive students will approach the teacher at the desk, but many students will not. Good teachers are unwilling to settle for that. Nor are they willing to leave untapped the rich educational opportunity presented to them during that period of time when students are concentrating on their own assignments.

DISCIPLINE

Effective teachers seldom experience problems with disruptive student behavior. For the most part, effective teachers have few discipline problems, largely because the way they manage their classrooms creates an environment and a learning experience for youngsters that keep students focused on the proper business of schools. If there are any "tricks" to successful discipline, they consist mostly of being successful in helping students learn the subject for which the teacher is responsible. Effective instructors have few discipline problems, not because they are "good disciplinarians," but because they are good teachers.

But no classroom, no teacher is immune from occasional behavior problems. Effective teachers consistently do at least two things when confronted by a potentially disruptive situation, and these are the same things many marginal teachers do not do.

First, an effective teacher is never cute with students. If a youngster needs to be corrected, the good teacher does it in as simple and straightforward a manner as possible. There is no elaborate sarcasm, no indirect references to "third grade behavior," and no effort made to deprive the student of his or her dignity. Teachers who are guilty of those behaviors invite adolescents to detest them and give the student the motive to "get even," because they've placed the student in a situation where the student must find some way to restore face with the peer group.

Second, an effective teacher senses immediately what corrective approach fits the situation that is developing, or has already developed. Often, the entire group suffers from an inexplicable but tangible restlessness or inattentiveness that seems pervasive. In other instances, nearly everyone in the classroom appears to be functioning effectively, but one or two students present distinct exceptions; they are operating ineffectively, or perhaps even disruptively.

The good teacher never confuses the basic difference between these two situations. When the entire group seems to be possessed by demons, the good teacher directs his or her remarks to the entire group. Individual students are not singled out for corrective action. Instead the teacher says something like, "Class, things are not working the way they're supposed to right at this moment, and we're going to have to get organized. I want each of you to settle down, because unless you do, we cannot proceed, and that simply won't do. Now, let's get going again so I don't have to interrupt you anymore."

When things are going well except for one or two students, the effective teacher employs an entirely different approach. In that situation the entire group is not the problem, and the teacher does not address remarks to the entire group. Instead the teacher moves right to the offender(s) and says directly and quietly to him/them, "Sam, you're not cooperating the way I expect you to. I want you to stop [whatever it is Sam's doing] and begin the assignment. Now show me some first-class behavior or else you and I will have a serious falling out."

The key to the effective handling of these disparate situations is to recognize quickly the basic difference in the characteristics of each, then to take the measure appropriate to the specific situation. The good teacher knows that one approach is right for a specific situation, but wrong for another. Like a physician, the skilled teacher prescribes the right medicine only after a correct diagnosis is made of the problem that needs attention. The teacher knows prescribing the wrong medicine may actually make the situation worse.

SUCCESS FOR STUDENTS

Perhaps one of the most important things outstanding teachers do is give their students--nearly all their students--a chance to be successful. Somewhere along the line they create an opportunity (even for their poorer students) for each youngster to say about an assignment, or project, or whatever, "I did that well!"

Effective teachers know instinctively that no one can live with satisfaction in any environment where he or she has never experienced anything even remotely resembling success. All of us hate to be made to do things we cannot do. Yet, many students spend week after week in school under precisely those circumstances.

Admittedly, the demands of some advanced courses in certain studies may simply overpower an individual student. In some cases the distractions of home or environmental circumstances may be so formidable for a student that school is perceived as a meaningless game. Still other youngsters may be handicapped in tangible or intangible ways to the extent that conventional classrooms simply do not provide a suitable learning environment.

With the possible exception of a few such youngsters, most students can achieve some satisfaction from a "conventional" class taken from a good teacher. The teacher sees to it, but admittedly it is hard work and requires a commitment some teachers feel they cannot make. The effective ones do.

The effective teacher doesn't give high grades away like gumdrops, but neither does he or she withhold them in deference to "maintaining my standards." When a student does a good job, no valid end is served by withholding from the student an appropriate grade. Grades should be awarded to reflect accurately the quality of work judged against a fair and realistic standard. Teachers who prate incessantly about being "hard graders" often have no other triumphs to cite.

Good teachers are also sensitive to the impact their written comments have upon students. Many students have mountains of negative comments about the quality of their work by the time the first semester is finished, and that's often all they have. But the effective teacher seeks opportunities, and they are sometimes very difficult to find, to praise periodically <u>something</u> about every student's work. These teachers are alert to even the faintest glimmer of hope in a student's efforts, and quickly comment positively about that feature.

Students have told me on many occasions about some positive comment made by a teacher that had caused them to perceive themselves differently—and more positively—than they had before. Frequently the encouragement and hope a student feels as a result of that comment from a teacher may be, at least for some students, the most

significant event of the month. Indeed the effects may
last longer than any other outcome of the class.

However, the best teachers do all this and then the
most difficult thing of all, in addition: they
periodically create assignments that present to each
student a reputable academic challenge the student is
capable of meeting successfully. Rather than devising,
for instance, one assignment to be handled in common by
all class members, these teachers, now and then when it
is suitable, develop differentiated assignments geared
to the talents and abilities of the different students
in their class. The assignments are all reputable,
legitimate assignments, but the levels of challenge they
present vary with the levels of ability of the class
members.

For the student who is perpetually faced with the
agony of defeat, the possibility of experiencing the
thrill of victory must be heady stuff indeed. All good
teachers try to make that opportunity available to all
students as often as possible.

A FINAL WORD

There is, of course, a great deal more than this
to being an effective teacher; much, much more. No
responsible educator would suggest there exists a bag
of tricks which, when mastered, guarantees successful
performance. In fact, the most important qualities may
be the most elusive, most intangible of all.

Among those qualities that mark effective secondary
school teachers is a thorough knowledge of, and love for,
the subject being taught. That, in turn, generates the
genuine enthusiasm those teachers demonstrate, but, more
than that, it also permits them the luxury of being
intellectually comfortable and assured as they assist
students who are confronting and trying to grasp the
intricacies of the discipline. Many of the desirable
behaviors identified in this chapter clearly will not
occur unless the teacher first has a deep understanding
of his or her discipline. Simply put, it is very
difficult to teach anyone anything if you don't first
understand it thoroughly yourself.

Another characteristic that marks master teachers
is that they genuinely like and enjoy other people--
including students. There are those, of course, who are

more comfortable with ideas or things than they are with people, and there's certainly nothing wrong with that. However, teachers necessarily function in a world where the entities that surround them are predominantly people, and the teachers who function best in that world are those who enjoy being with others, both adults and students. Again, much of what has been written in this chapter implies that.

Finally, the best teachers I know are professionals in the best sense of that word. They take pride in their performance and consistently set standards for themselves that are far more taxing than would be necessary if their purpose were simply to get by. To be sure, they periodically grouse and complain like the rest of us, but when they walk into their classrooms they are dedicated professionals, committed to maintaining the fierce and justifiable, if quiet, pride in performance that distinguishes their work.

It should perhaps be said, too, that these good teachers, who have been the subject of this chapter, would be the first to suggest that it does not do to get too caught up in a close analysis of all dimensions of the teaching-learning act. They believe, as I do, that when all the analysts and theorists have had their say, good teaching remains more art than science. Master teachers are indeed artists, artists who have mastered the craft their profession requires.

REFERENCES AND SUGGESTED READINGS
Amidon, Edward, and Hunter, Elizabeth. Improving Teaching. Chicago: Holt, Rinehart and Winston, 1966.
Aylesworth, Thomas G., and Reagan, Gerald M. Teaching for Thinking. Garden City, N.Y.: Doubleday, 1969.
Bruner, Jerome S. The Process of Education. New York: Random House, 1960.
Dunn, Rita, and Dunn, Kenneth. Teaching Students through Their Individual Learning Styles. Englewood Cliffs, N.J.: Prentice-Hall, 1978.
Henderson, George, and Bibens, Robert F. Teachers Should Care. New York: Harper & Row, 1970.
Hunter, Madeline. "The Learning Process." In Dwight Allen and Eli Siefman, eds. The Teacher's Handbook. Glenview, Ill.: Scott, Foresman, 1971.

Hunter, Madeline. "The Teaching Process." In Dwight
    Allen and Eli Siefman, eds. The Teacher's
    Handbook. Glenview, Ill.: Scott, Foresman, 1971.
Keefe, James W., ed. Student Learning Styles. Reston,
    Va.: National Association of Secondary School
    Principals, 1979.
Sanders, Norris M. Classroom Questions. New York:
    Harper & Row, 1966.
Shumsky, Abraham. In Search of Teaching Style. New
    York: Appleton-Century-Crofts, 1968.

6

CURRICULUM DECISION MAKING

L. James Walter

Curriculum writers, in models they create, indicate it is the people as represented by schoolboards who have the ultimate authority for deciding curricula. Broad curriculum goals are decided by local boards of education and these goals determine the nature of the overall curricula for the entire school system. However, teachers frequently define specific curricula in special disciplines and for particular groups of students.

CURRICULUM DECISIONS

The curriculum decisions for which teachers are largely responsible can be categorized into two general types, departmental or program decisions, and classroom decisions. The first two types are generally made by small groups of teachers; the latter types are made by individual teachers. When schools make extensive use of team teaching, classroom curriculum decisions are made by a small group of teachers—the team.

Decisions regarding what is to be taught to students are most commonly expressed in terms of goals and objectives. Goals are general statements about what students should know, do, or feel after they have been instructed. An example of a goal in science would be: the student will understand the concepts of living and nonliving matter. Objectives, often derived from goals, are specific statements about students' abilities to know, do, or feel following instruction. An example of an objective for the goal stated previously would be: classify given cells into these categories: plants, animals, and protists. Explain how you classified the cells by describing the principal cell structures that distinguish them. Goals are long-range statements-- objectives are short-range statements.

Sources of potential goals can be many but it may be useful to think of three primary sources. First, the students themselves are a source. The needs students have and the interests they express are rich sources for determining goals and, eventually, the curriculum. Major diagnoses of student needs and interests for determining potential goals for the entire curriculum is the responsibility of central office administrators in a school district, whereas classroom teachers may use student needs and interests to determine classroom level objectives and determine the sequence and timing of certain specific topics.

A second area of potential goals stems from societal needs. Societal trends and problems are major factors influencing the curriculum. Career education, current events studies, and selection of various pieces of literature are examples of societal influence on the curriculum. Many school districts have used a formal needs assessment process to collect information from their patrons regarding perceived societal needs.

Finally, the formal subject disciplines are also sources of curriculum goals. The focus here is on transmitting the best of the cultural heritage from one generation to the next. This was the principal focus of the school curriculum in the early part of this century. One may ask: What is so important and valuable in this discipline that it should be taught to large numbers of students? To answer the question with wisdom, one must really have mastered the content in a discipline and know its structure.

So, as we have seen, the needs and interests of students, societal needs, and subject disciplines are three general sources of curriculum goals. Which source should have priority? Areas of curriculum mathematics, vocational education, English, and the like, focus on goals derived from one source more than others. I believe that in the overall curriculum we should strive for a balance of goals derived from all three sources. At various times in a student's career, different areas should be emphasized.

The impact of the federal and state governments has been dramatic. The federal government has mandated school programs for handicapped students and provided money for everything from hot lunch programs to innovative programs for gifted students. The amount of influence of the federal government varies widely from school district to school district. Districts that choose to request federal funds are obligated to meet federal guidelines. Programs for the handicapped are mandated through legislation now referred to primarily by number, 94-142. Other examples of federal influence would be Title IX, sexual equality; and Title I programs, programs for disadvantaged students.

State governments also exert influence over the curricula of local school districts. In states where there exists a tradition of strong state government, the state generally has more influence on the schools than in states where the state government is less strong. In the Midwest, states seem to have less influence over local school curricula than exists on either the East Coast or West Coast. Some states dictate specific courses that must be offered. Others describe general guidelines which schools must meet to qualify for state aid funds. One could generally conclude that the higher the state's contribution to the overall cost of running the schools, the more influence the state government exercises over the schools.

DECISIONS TEACHERS MUST MAKE

The teaching assignment determines in large part the range of curricular and instructional decisions a teacher must make. Below is a list of possible decisions teachers will need to make and they are sequenced chronologically as they affect the school year. Not every teacher will have to make each decision, but here is a possible list:

1. What exactly should I teach the students?
2. How should I organize the course or subject?
3. What materials do I have to serve as resources for me?
4. What resources will I need for students to use?
5. How can I capture the students' attention?
6. What other instructional resources are available?
7. How will I know whether I have the teaching ability to get the student results I desire?
8. Will my learning activities fill the allocated time? (This is a primary concern of most beginning teachers.)
9. How should I evaluate student progress?

10. Which teaching models are most appropriate for the objectives and the students?
11. How can I get students to be active rather than passive?
12. Can I tell how things are going during the lessons or class?
13. How can I accommodate to the individual needs of students?
14. Will I be able to see success when it happens?

If beginning teachers could answer each of these questions for each unit they taught--indeed, if experienced teachers could always answer such questions--they should be moved to the top of the salary schedule. Presenting the fourteen questions was done to show the number and range of decisions to be made. As a teacher gains experience and acquires additional instructional materials, making such decisions becomes much easier. It has often been said that the first year of teaching is the most difficult. I would have to agree. Beginning teachers often have extremely high expectations for themselves and their students. This is a quality that is to be encouraged. As with any profession, once a teacher learns the nature of the job and gains an understanding of the priority tasks in teaching, the job becomes easier--not easy, but easier.

MODELS FOR DECISION MAKING
     Two ways of thinking about planning curriculum may be helpful. The first is called the <u>Ends-Means Model</u> and the second is called the <u>Means-Ends Model</u>.
     The Ends-Means Model, illustrated in Figure 6.1,

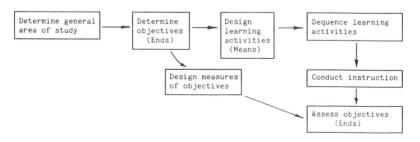

Fig. 6.1 The Ends-Means Model of Instructional Planning

begins with determining what the ends of instruction
will be for a group of students. These ends are most
commonly written in the form of performance objectives.
Next, the planner determines measures or test items for
each objective and follows the step with selection and
organization of learning activities, or means.

The Means-Ends Model, illustrated in Figure 6.2,
has many of the same steps as listed in the previous
model. The principal difference is the point at which
one begins the planning process. Using this model, the
teacher designs the learning activities without first
determining the objectives. After instruction has taken
place the teacher decides the material over which students
are to be tested and designs the test measures.

Which model is better? I believe that the Ends-Means
Model is the most systematic and efficient to use because
it is a model that focuses instructional resources toward
predetermined student objectives. It also allows students
to know what is expected prior to instruction so that
they can sort out important elements from lesser important
ones during instruction. However, research seems to
indicate that teachers prefer to use the Means-Ends Model
to plan their instruction. They don't as a group follow
the formal process of stating performance objectives
before they begin to teach. The reasons for this could
include time constraints, lack of skill in writing
objectives, and/or philosophical opposition to the
process. New teachers are free to select the model
preferred--experienced teachers are free to change models
should they find one better than the other. If an area
of teaching is easily defined and organized by definite
sets of skills, writing performance objectives may be

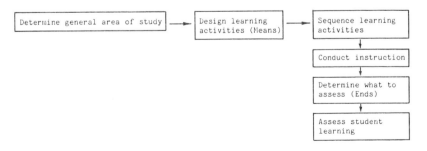

Fig. 6.2 The Means-Ends Model of Instructional
Planning

an appropriate process to follow. On the other hand,
if the teacher views the teaching areas as open and
dynamic, he or she may prefer to provide some stimulating
experiences and then determine later what students should
have learned.

LEARNING EXPERIENCES
        In his book, Human Characteristics and School
Learning, Benjamin Bloom states that the most important
instructional factor in student learning is how active
the learner is in the learning process. So the essential
guideline is to keep the students active. One can
generalize the principle by saying that the more active
learners are in the process the more they are learning.
        In the Ends-Means Model of planning, learning
activities can be determined by looking at objectives.
One might ask: What should students do to meet objectives
of instruction? The key to using this model is to match
objectives (ends) and activities (means). As a guideline,
teachers may wish to have students practice the ends
stated in the objectives before the instruction is over.

SEQUENCING LEARNING EXPERIENCES
        Learning theories are as plentiful as learning
theorists and too often the prospective teacher is
overwhelmed by seeming contradictions. Perhaps the best
guidelines for sequencing learning experiences could be
found in A. M. Kilgore's thoughts on models of teaching
and teaching strategies, found in Chapter 7. Kilgore's
notion is that a teacher should try to match objectives
with appropriate teaching models or parts of teaching
models. Following this step, a teacher should blend the
models together to form an overall teaching strategy for
a unit of instruction. Blending the different models
into a strategy is not a scientific task--it is artistic
and largely intuitive. Experienced teachers who have
attempted the task find it stimulating and creative.
By using such an approach, teachers can take advantage
of the research of many learning theorists and provide
instructional variety for the students.

INDIVIDUALIZING INSTRUCTION
        During the past twenty-five years much has been
written about individualizing instruction. Individualized

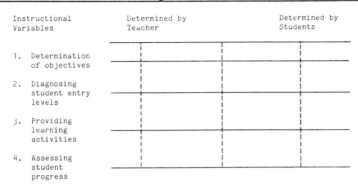

Instructional Variables	Determined by Teacher	Determined by Students
1. Determination of objectives		
2. Diagnosing student entry levels		
3. Providing learning activities		
4. Assessing student progress		

Fig. 6.3 A Matrix for Individualized Instruction

instruction can be thought of as an extension of the Ends-Means Model, and viewed as being on a continuum from being teacher-determined to being student-determined. The matrix in Figure 6.3 below should be of help in organizing data.

If a teacher uses a common set of objectives for all students, gives them the same instruction and tests at the same time, is this an example of individualized instruction? According to the matrix it is, provided all students are ready for the instruction. As a teacher makes students increasingly responsible for particular instructional components, the degree of individualized instruction is increased. A teacher who gives great amounts of responsibility to students for planning, conducting, and evaluating their own instruction is moving students toward independent learning, a goal many school districts have established.

EXPECTATIONS OF STUDENTS

What teachers expect for students is extremely idiosyncratic. A sound practice can result from having several teachers who have similar assignments work cooperatively to determine common expectations. Various requirements are thus discussed and the teachers provide a firm rationale for the requirements. Of course, many teachers already have had success doing this.

Teachers entering the profession now will find schools increasing their expectations of students. Evidence of this is found in new competency tests, increased graduation requirements, fewer electives, and

more rigorous evaluations of student performance in almost
every area of the curriculum.

Some considerations for determining expectations
are summarized below:

1. Age and previous educational background of students.
2. Statements of expectations found in curriculum guides
   and course syllabi.
3. Nature of the subject or course. Is the course an
   elective? Is the course a prerequisite for another
   course?
4. Overall, what value is placed on the course by the
   faculty and the community? In general, faculties
   and the community have very high expectations for
   student success in reading, mathematics, and, most
   of all, in writing.

Determining appropriate expectations for student
performance takes time. Teachers should be reasonable
during the first two or three years of teaching until
they have a clearer idea of what students can do. The
more clearly teachers communicate their expectations to
students, the better the chance students will have of
obtaining them. As teachers become more experienced in
knowing what to expect of students and telling them, they
can begin to increase their expectations.

EVALUATING INSTRUCTIONAL EFFECTIVENESS

In areas of teaching where student outcomes are
clearly defined, determining the effectiveness of the
instructional program is a simpler task than it is in
areas where outcomes are not so clear. In other words,
teachers of algebra have an easier time in assessing the
relative success of their programs than a teacher in
American studies.

Teachers are constantly receiving feedback from
students. Formal tests provide concrete evidence of
student learning and these can serve as primary evidence
that the instructional program is an effective one.
Informal data are also a good indication of the success
of the program. Students' enthusiasm, students' ability
to stay "on task," and students' attitudes toward learning
serve as immediate cues of a program's success.

For beginning teachers, there exists a tendency to

be too sensitive to student informal feedback and to make changes while students are still engaged in the activity. This can be a mistake. Once a plan is made, an inexperienced teacher should not make sweeping changes until the entire unit or segment is completed. After the instruction is over and formal assessments of student progress are made, better decisions regarding modifications can be made. A teacher may want to sample student attitudes formally at the end of the instructional sequence and use this information in making subsequent decisions.

Sources other than student evaluation can be used to determine overall instructional effectiveness, such as self-evaluation, administrator or peer evaluation, and parent evaluation. Each has some advantages and disadvantages:

1. Self-evaluation. This form of evaluation can be very effective but objectivity can be a problem. A teacher must have a model or reference point in mind when using a self-evaluation approach. Part of the plan could include making a videotape of a typical teaching performance and later analyzing it by comparing it with a selected model.
2. Administrator or peer evaluation. Most schools have some form of administrator evaluation, particularly of untenured teachers. If done properly, information can be very helpful in changing teacher behavior. In order to be helpful, information from administrators or peers must provide specific data and include teaching concepts that the teacher values. Peer observation can be very helpful for beginning teachers because the threat of administrator evaluation can be eliminated. It is important, however, to provide training for the peer observers.
3. Parent evaluation. This source of information has been used successfully, particularly in the elementary schools. (However, the type of information collected from parents should be approved by the school administrator.) Parents can provide insights into student reactions to instructional events that may be more valid than student reactions alone. This is especially true for programs involving younger students.

REFERENCES AND SUGGESTED READINGS
Bloom, Benjamin. Human Characteristics and School
    Learning. New York: McGraw-Hill, 1976.
Joyce, Bruce R., and Weil, Marsha. Models of Teaching.
    2d ed. Englewood Cliffs, N.J.: Prentice-Hall, 1980.
McNeil, John D. Curriculum: A Comprehensive
    Introduction. 2d ed. Boston: Little, Brown,
    1981.
Saylor, Galen D., et al. Curriculum Planning for Better
    Teaching and Learning. New York: Holt, Rinehart
    and Winston, 1981.

7

STRATEGIES OF TEACHING

Alvah M. Kilgore

Teachers often are compared to artists: a teacher creates an environment that is unique, much like an artist who creates a unique sculpture or painting.

The artist and the teacher learn to work with the tools of their professions. Training programs and professional courses attempt to help both teachers and artists learn some of the techniques, methods, and skills of their profession, and generally provide some time for the novices to practice in their prospective fields.

THE ART OF THE SCIENCE OF TEACHING

To try to understand more about teaching and learning and what constitutes master teaching, continual efforts are being made to describe it in terms of research. Results from such research are sometimes referred to as the science of teaching and most teacher training programs include valid research findings. Effective teachers, once they know about the results of research, can take these scientific findings, add them to their teaching repertoire, and create a more effective--artistic --environment for the students.

WHAT RESEARCH TELLS US

Process-Product Research

Two major research thrusts have provided us with usable information. The first centers around what is called process-product research which looks at outcomes

of learning, for example, standardized test scores, and/or
student attitudes. College board test scores or results
from other standardized tests provide information that
allows comparisons to be made among schools, grade levels,
subject areas, and teachers. After choosing scores that
are consistently high in a given area, a researcher can
identify the teachers and classrooms from which these
scores were obtained. The researcher can then try to
find out what teachers are doing that might be bringing
about the higher scores. This cause (teaching process)
and effect (student product) relationship has provided
us with some generalized, useful information about
teaching and learning:

1. There is no one best way to teach. Some general
   skills can be used by all teachers; some teaching
   behaviors should be avoided by all teachers. However,
   a few universal behaviors or skills can be used by
   all teachers in all classroom situations.

2. Teachers, especially when beginning to teach a new
   subject or course, will, by a trial and error process,
   work until a successful teaching pattern (for them)
   has been developed. They then tend to use that
   pattern for all students.

3. Teaching patterns can be classified into two major
   categories. One is called direct teaching, wherein
   the teacher provides new or additional information
   to students in a number of ways (that is, by
   lecturing, showing a film or filmstrip, or taking
   a field trip). The second pattern is known as
   indirect teaching. In this pattern the teacher
   structures activities in which the learner is active
   (as opposed to passive in the direct teaching sense)
   and involved in a variety of situations, such as
   playing games, group role playing, inquiry training,
   and laboratory work.

4. Effective teachers are flexible and try to blend
   direct and indirect types of teaching behavior when
   planning and teaching an instructional unit. The
   degree of directness and indirectness is often related
   to grade level and subject being taught. For example,
   in elementary mathematics and language skills,
   effective teachers use direct types of teaching.
   In intermediate level reading classes and most
   secondary school subjects, successful

teachers use a combination of direct-indirect teaching behaviors.
5. Successful teachers continue to learn new skills and are able to adapt new methods or models of teaching into their existing teaching repertoire.

Aptitude-Treatment-Interaction (ATI)

A second and more recent research thrust centers around the interaction between how teachers teach and how students learn. This type of research is called aptitude-treatment-interaction or ATI. Within this framework, two major divisions have developed. One division concerns the identification of behavioral characteristics of both teacher and student and how they affect one another in the classroom. For example, one characteristic is the need for structure. Some people (both teachers and students) need a lot of structure, others need a minimum. The research question is: What happens when a teacher with a low structure profile is teaching a group of students who have a high structure need? This type of research is in its infancy and has not yet produced enough information for us to develop generalizations applicable to teaching.

The second division of ATI research, however, has proven to be very valuable for adding to a teacher's repertoire of effective teaching practices. Additionally, strong ties have been noted between the results of this research and student learning. In fact, it has proved to be one of the most exciting concepts to occur in the last twenty years of educational research. We call the results of this research, teaching models.

TEACHING MODELS

This research was primarily developed by individuals whose major interests were centered on how pupils learn rather than discovering how to teach more effectively. The researchers (who generally worked independently of one another) developed some theories of how students learn and then tested their theories in laboratories and classrooms. Once they discovered what appeared to work, they devised systematic sequences of behaviors that teachers should follow in order to produce the same effects that had appeared in their research models. Over eighty such models or programs have been identified, each

purporting to have the answer to meeting students'
learning needs.

Over a period of several years the federal government
sponsored the research and development of several of these
teaching models by providing research grants to the
theorists who were developing these techniques.
Ultimately, the question was raised as to the
identification of the behaviors of effective teachers.
An educational researcher, Bruce Joyce, received a federal
grant to find the answer. After two years of visitations,
consultations, readings, and talks with a variety of
educators and researchers, Joyce published a book, Models
of Teaching. This book is a benchmark in modern
education in that it conceptualized and organized these
models of teaching into a comprehensive yet understandable
work that is changing the way American teachers teach.

Additionally, since the publication of the original
book, a series of self-instructional paperback books by
Weil and Joyce, on models of teaching, have become
available to educators. These books describe, in step-by-
step sequence, the process by which a teacher can learn
to use a specific model of teaching. Since these
resources are available, I will not attempt to duplicate
them in this chapter. Rather, I will share a process
by which a teacher can use all the resources at his or
her command and organize them into a productive teaching
sequence. The resources to be used include the content
to be taught; the available materials and aids; knowledge
of the students and selection of learning activities; and
teaching skills, methods, and models. I call this process
the development of a teaching strategy.

I have been developing and using this concept over
the past few years. Practicing teachers have been working
with me throughout the developmental stages and the sample
(described later in this chapter) is a product of many
hours of suggestions and input as to how to use this
process most effectively. Teachers have been generally
pleased with their strategies (each one differs) and their
ability to document both personal as well as pupil growth.

A teaching strategy is somewhat analogous to a
general's battle plan or a coach's game plan. A strategy
is much larger than a daily lesson plan and more inclusive
than a curriculum unit plan. A strategy calls for a
teacher to predetermine a series of desired pupil outcomes
within an instructional sequence, and then to weave all

the appropriate resources needed to accomplish those ends into a plan that will accomplish the intended outcomes. A strategy is a process by which the teacher creates an "artistic design," using scientific information, into a "painting" that is singularly unique to that teacher and his or her students.

Generally, when planning, teachers have some notions of goals and objectives they are seeking and a well-developed comprehension of their subject matter and available materials. A strategy includes these important elements but also asks the teacher to include learning activities and the appropriate teaching method or model. As the models of teaching are the critical new element in a strategy, it is important to understand how a model might offset a learner and a learning sequence.

Using Teaching Models

Since models of teaching are based on theories of how students learn, a learning theorist will list, after a model has been researched, the steps a teacher should use to attain the desired learner outcomes. All the many models of teaching are designed to accomplish certain learner outcomes. Effective teachers have learned to use a variety of teaching techniques to allow all students to acquire what they want them to learn, since teachers now recognize that students learn differently. Some students learn best by listening and watching and inquiring, others need personal attention, and still others learn better by social interaction. The important concept to remember is that the wider a repertoire of teaching skills and models a teacher has at his or her command, the greater the chance of more students achieving the intended learning goals.

Teaching styles can be categorized into two major areas, direct and indirect teaching, as defined in point 4 earlier in this chapter. These categories are not designed to be evaluative, but rather consist of general descriptive behavior with which a teacher can identify. Most effective teachers structure and use both direct and indirect teaching. Overuse of any single teaching model or style by a teacher is ineffective and has given teaching a bad name. The lecture model is a notorious example of poor teaching. While it is not in and of itself poor, the overuse of this model has contributed to its reputation. On the other hand, learners need

information. The lecture method is an efficient way to
provide this information but certainly not the only way.
Additionally, those that advocate experiential and inquiry
modes of learning sometimes forget that one cannot inquire
in a vacuum. One needs to have some information in order
to ask the appropriate questions.

Teachers can readily categorize their teaching by
simply reviewing the types of activities they engaged
in during their past teaching episodes as a currently
employed teacher, substitute teacher, or student teacher.
If in primarily a direct mode, he or she provided verbal
and other passive learning experiences in the classroom;
if in a more indirect series of activities, the student
roles were active in group situations such as inquiry
training or laboratory sessions.

MODEL FAMILIES
        Each of the major models of teaching has identified
primary and secondary student outcomes, and has been
placed in model families; that is, clusters of teaching
models are grouped according to similarity of purposes.
The three families of models are first, the information
processing family, with models designed for students
who best learn through cognitive or intellectual
facilities. The second family is designed for students
who learn best through social interaction, and the third
is designed for those who need personalized learning
experiences. It is with these thoughts in mind that the
following synthesis of the models of teaching is offered.
Also remember that even though I have stated the primary
outcome of a family of models, each model within the
family offers variations on a theme. Each family will
be followed by a short description of how a model or two
might be used.

Information Processing Family

Information Processing Models
        Primary purposes: To learn factual materials,
develop concepts and generalizations, enhance academic
skills and higher-level thinking skills--primarily in
the cognitive domain.
        Secondary purposes: To provide alternative ways
to gather and process information. With the indirect

models, to enhance social interaction and group process skills.

Direct Models	Indirect Models
1. Oral Presentation	1. Concept Attainment (Bruner)
a. explanations	
b. direction-giving	2. Concept Development (Taba)
c. new information	
d. opinions (values)	3. Inquiry Training (Suchman)
2. Demonstration	
a. how-to-do-it process	4. Advanced Organizer (Ausubel)
b. science experiments	
c. use of new materials	5. Development (Piaget)
d. safety procedures	6. Cause-Effect (Taba)
e. psychomotor skills	7. Application of Generalizations (Taba)
3. Sensory Assimilation	
a. films/filmstrips	8. Recitation
b. television programs	
c. field trips	
d. recordings/tapes	
4. Individualized Instruction	
a. Individually Prescribed Instruction (IPI)	
b. Individually Guided Education (IGE)	
c. Programmed texts	
d. Individual Educational Planning (IEP)	

Mrs. Woods, a mathematics teacher, has asked her students to read a chapter in the text about uses of the metric system and shown a film, Measurement around the World (direct models, sensory assimilation). She would like to determine what the students learned and how they conceptualized information about the metric system. She chooses to use the concept development model (indirect models, cause-effect, Taba) and asks the students to recall all the information they remembered about the reading and the film (Step 1); cluster or group their items based on similarities (Step 2); label or name the groups (Step 3); and prioritize or subsume items and groups (Step 4). The results of this model provided

answers to the questions of what the students remembered,
how they organized their information, and how they
determined degrees of importance. Her next activities
might be to divide the class into task groups and use
inquiry training (indirect models, inquiry training,
Suchman) to solve metric system problems.

Social Interaction Family

Social Interaction Models
Primary purposes: To develop interpersonal and group
process skills, to learn and apply social values, to
increase students' ability to relate to others, and to
develop group problem solving abilities.
Secondary purposes: To nurture creativity, academic
awareness, development of concepts, application of factual
materials, and further development of academic skills.
To also serve as motivators for a variety of learning
activities.

Direct Models	Indirect Models
By our definition, no social models of teaching are connected with direct teaching.	1. Process Training (Mallan)
	2. Jurisprudential (Oliver and Shaver)
	3. Group Investigation (Thelan)
	4. Role Playing (Shaftel)
	5. Social Inquiry (Massialas)
	6. Simulation (Boocock)
	7. Classroom Meeting (Glasser)

Miss Grimes, an English teacher who also teaches
journalism and is responsible for the school paper, has
run into a problem concerning censorship with her senior
students. Since no clear-cut policy on censorship had
been established, she decided to have the students develop
and test a policy. She wrote a short case study and,
using the jurisprudential indirect model, presented the
case to the class (Step 1). The class clarified the facts
in the case, identified the issues, and developed some
public policy statements (Step 2). Students then were
asked to take a position regarding the policy statement

(Step 3). Time was allowed for students to explore their positions in depth, gather data, interview others, and argue their position with others in the class (Step 4). After arguments, the time for refining and qualifying positions was given and the students learned to shift and modify, and perhaps come closer to some resolution, especially after some pointed questioning by the teacher (Step 5). Finally, the new policy was reality tested prior to full implementation as students predicted what might happen if the policy was used (Step 6). Final refinements were then made and the class had an operational plan.

Personalized Learning Family

Personalized Learning Models

Primary purposes: To learn through self-understanding, creativity, personal values orientation, and an increased sensitivity toward others through self-actualization.

Secondary purposes: To nurture awareness in others, help solve problems, act as motivators for developing academic skills and concepts, as well as further refinement and development of social interaction skills.

Direct Models	Indirect Models
1. Expository: Depends on pupil's ability to read a variety of materials that he or she can personally relate to-- also implies a teacher's ability to write clearly.	1. Nondirective Teaching (Rogers)
	2. Synectics (Gordon)
	3. Values Clarification (Raths, Simon)
2. Some individualized education may be classified here if an opportunity is provided for a teacher to diagnose and prescribe from a variety of sources.	4. T-Group Training (NTL Labs)
	5. Awareness Training (Perls)

Note: Although the models are described as personalized, many may take place within a group setting and some require group interaction. These models become

personalized when a student takes what has been learned
and makes applications to his or her personal projects
and behaviors.

Students in Mr. Dudley's English class were asked
to write a descriptive essay on the possible feelings
of presidential candidates on the night before the
presidential election (direct models, expository). As
he moved around the room, Dudley noticed that the
descriptions the students were writing seemed dull and
unimaginative. He then chose to use the synectics model
(Indirect, Gordon). This model attempts to have students
begin to look at events or people in new and creative
ways by using metaphors and analogies. He stopped the
writing and asked the students to verbally describe some
of what they had written (Step 1). The students were
asked to then compare the candidates' feelings to some
nonliving objects, such as a switchboard or a lump of
clay. Once the students had listed several direct
analogies (Step 2), they chose one (a ferris wheel), and
became that item. They described how they might look,
act, and feel (Step 3, personal analogy). The students
then chose words from their personal and direct analogies
that were in conflict with each other, such as dreary
and bright, and listed them in a different group (Step
4, compressed conflict). Students chose one-word pairs
and developed new direct analogies (Step 5). They then
used these new analogies to write about how the candidates
might have felt on election eve (Step 6). The essays
were much more enjoyable and creative after completion
of this activity.

PLANNING A TEACHING STRATEGY
        It is not my purpose to advocate a set of teaching
skills or to instruct in the ability to operationalize
several models of teaching. I assume readers already
have an abundance of skills and if they want to learn
to use additional teaching models the resources are
available. My purpose is to share a strategy planning
process wherein teachers may more efficiently organize
what they are currently doing with strategic format for
improving their classroom instruction.
        The prerequisites to planning a teaching strategy
are:

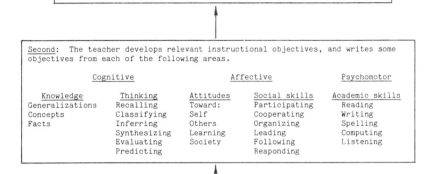

Fig. 7.1 A Teacher Decision Making Matrix:
Relationship of the Necessary Elements in a Teaching
Strategy

1. Identification of school goals
2. Awareness of departmental, subject area, or grade
    level goals
3. Ability to write relevant instructional objectives
    for a curriculum unit
4. Content knowledge
5. Content materials
6. A variety of teaching skills and models

The teacher decision making matrix (Figure 7.1)
illustrates the relationship of these elements in a
teaching strategy. The matrix can be used in helping
teachers decide what elements to include in their
strategies. Remember, a strategy is generally analogous
to a curriculum unit. The major difference is that the

strategy is much more inclusive and prescriptive in terms
of students' achievements of the objectives.
    Figure 7.2 is a teaching strategy completed by a
junior high English teacher and is an example of how the
strategy parts fit together. Refer to Figure 7.2 as you
read through the directions.

SPECIFIC PROCEDURES FOR THE USE OF THE DECISION MAKING
MATRIX

Part I. Objectives and Rationale
1. Identify the content topic or area to be the strategy
    focus and state it in terms of a title.
2. Identify and write the school or curricular goals
    that will be the overall focus of the strategy, and
    to which the objectives will be related.
3. Write anticipated pupil outcome objectives, include
    who is to do what, under what conditions, and to what
    degree of accuracy the objectives should be attained.
    The objectives should, in some way, be measurable.
    Use the teacher decision making chart as a focal point
    for developing the objectives. Include objectives
    from the cognitive and affective domains. These
    should describe what a student will be able to do
    upon completion of the strategy.
4. Write a rationale for utilizing the specific content
    topic, materials used, and the relationship to other
    teaching strategies. This area justifies what the
    teacher is planning to do with students in the
    classroom.

Part II. Development of the Activity Sequence
    The intention behind the sequence of activities is
the assumption that when the students complete the planned
activities the outcome objectives should be reached.
Activity numbers do not signify lessons and/or days.
A single activity may take three consecutive days, or
one class session may include two or more activities.
The intent behind each activity is that it contributes
to objective attainment by pupils. Therefore, the
activity must be consistent with the intended outcome
objectives.

1. Activity Purpose. This section creates a situation
    in which the teacher states the reason for the

Fig. 7.2   Teaching Strategy Planning Form

School	Junior High
Grade	8
Subject	English (Basic Studies)
	Thematic unit on law and
	justice based on novel,
	Harper Lee, To Kill a
	Mockingbird

Part I Objectives and Rationale
1. Title: The study of theme(s) and concepts present in Harper Lee, To Kill a Mockingbird
2. Related to Goals: Continued development of reading, thinking, writing, and discussion skills in addition to gaining further understanding of what students can learn about people, and specifically about themselves, through literature
3. Objectives Designed to Meet the Goals:
    (a) The student will demonstrate, to the satisfaction of the teacher, an attitude of willingness to share feelings about the characters and incidents present in the novel.
    (b) The student will demonstrate, to the satisfaction of the teacher, a willingness to cooperate in independent study assignments, small-group work, and total class activities.
    (c) Students will display knowledge of facts and concepts from the book, class activities, and discussions by correctly answering at least 70% of the questions on a test covering these materials. In addition each student will:
        (1) Write the attributes of the concepts justice and prejudice.
        (2) Write the major elements of fiction (characters, setting, plot, and point of view) and state how each of these is presented in this novel. This exercise is related to the Target: Writing unit, "Write to recall detail of fact and event."
    (d) The student will write satisfactorily a brief dialogue between himself/herself and either Jem or Scout after reading the book. (Target: Writing unit, "Write to give form to imaginative content.")
    (e) The student will orally state, to the satisfaction of the teacher, an idea of how life in the 1930s was both similar to and different from life in the 1970s.
4. Rationale: (Why are these objectives important?) Reading and responding to literature can give students a better understanding of people in society and of themselves. To Kill a Mockingbird is highly acclaimed and is part of the suggested 8th grade curriculum.
        The analysis of the major elements of fiction serves as reinforcement for other teaching strategies focusing on novels used this year. Also, the fact that To Kill a Mockingbird is set in the Depression is reinforcement for a previously studied Social Studies unit on the Depression at which time the English classes read the novel No Promises in the Wind by Irene Hunt.
        Learning to display a willingness to cooperate and participate develops in the students social skills which are beneficial to them in the future.

Part II Development of the Activity Sequence

Activity #	1. Activity Purpose	2. Expected Pupil Behaviors
1.	Allow students to recall previously learned facts about the Depression.	Students recall, group, label, and subsume what they remember of the Depression era.
2.	Provide students with a concept of justice.	Students internalize the concept of justice by being able to state the attributes of it.
3.	Provide students with a concept of prejudice.	Students internalize the concept of prejudice by being able to state the attributes of it.
4.	Allow students to review the major elements of fiction.	Students recall the major elements of fiction.
5.	Give students an overview of why we are studying this book.	Students listen, take notes, and ask questions.
6.	Provide an opportunity for students to read the book.	Students read the book.
7.	Allow students to explore feelings.	Students role play the deliberation of the jury at Tom Robinson's trial (especially when Mr. Cunningham is persuaded to change his vote to "guilty").
8.	Allow students to see Boo Radley in another way.	Students create words and phrases to describe Boo Radley.
9.	Give students the opportunity to make a decision.	Students make a decision about their opinions in response to the question: Should Atticus have been more aggressive in dealing with the people who mistreated him and his family because he was defending Tom Robinson?
10.	Provide students an opportunity to recall how the elements of fiction are presented in this novel.	Students write the major elements of fiction as they are presented in this novel.
11.	Allow students to explore values, attitudes, and perceptions.	Students role play the townspeople in the story and share their feelings about whether or not Boo had been treated fairly in his life.
12.	Allow students to "give form to imaginative content" (8th grade Target: Writing unit).	Each student writes a brief dialogue between himself/herself and either Jem or Scout.
13.	Allow students to draw conclusions based on what they have read.	Students discuss similarities and differences between the ways of life in the 1930s and the 1970s.
14.	Allow students to recall facts from the story.	Students complete a crossword puzzle as a review.
15.	Give students the opportunity to watch a videotape of the movie version and to discuss the similarities and differences between the movie and the book.	Students watch a videotape of To Kill a Mockingbird and discuss the similarities between the movie and the book.
16.	Evaluate student learning.	Students complete a written test with 70% accuracy.
17.	Provide students with feedback about the work they did on their tests.	Students look at their corrected tests and ask any questions they may have.

3. Planned Teacher Behavior Models

4. Materials

Concept Development
Steps 1-4. Focus on question: What do you
 know about the Depression?

Butcher paper, magic marker

Concept Attainment
(Selection-oriented)

Examples and nonexamples of the concept

Concept Attainment
(Reception-oriented)

Examples and nonexamples of the concept

Concept Development
Steps 1-3. Teacher lists student answers on
 the board.
Oral Presentation

Chalkboard, chalk

Oral Presentation
Directions; (give the assignment).
Role Playing
Videotape it.

Books

Videotape camera and recorder

Synectics

Jurisprudential
Social issue: What should be the role of
 the legal profession in cases of prejudice?
 Should a lawyer take a case if he/she
 doesn't believe in the accused?

Butcher paper, tape to display each
 phase of model around room
Chalkboard, scratch paper

Advanced Organizer
Review and follow-up activity #4.

Worksheets

Role Playing
(With process observers)

Role playing cards

Oral Presentation
 a. Review dialogue form.
 b. Give writing assignment.
Classroom Meeting

Examples of dialogue on transparencies

Prepare crossword puzzle. Give assignment.

Duplicated copies of the crossword puzzle

Show videotape. Conduct informal class
 discussion of the similarities and
 differences.

Videotape camera and player recorder

Prepare test. Administer test.

Tests

Correct tests. Explain answers sought.
 Make grade adjustments.

particular activity. This reason provides the
direction for stating learner behaviors and choosing
the appropriate teaching behavior (model) to
accomplish the learner behavior.

2. Expected Pupil Behaviors. This section specifies
the skills and/or pupil needs prerequisite to the
accomplishment of the objectives. In developing this
sequence, ask the question: What does the pupil
need to know (or do) in order to complete the
objectives? When these have been determined, place
these prerequisite behaviors in a series of
activities. The pupil behavior should be stated in
an objective format. This is usually an enabling
objective and does not necessarily require a
measurement factor.

3. Planned Teacher Behavior. This specifies the
instructional approaches needed to bring about the
pupil prerequisite skills and/or behaviors, and
ultimately the overall objectives. The choice of
teacher behavior is made based upon several factors
that must be considered. One, of course, is
preference of the teacher. The second is centered
around choosing the teaching model that best gets
the task accomplished.

   To aid in choosing appropriate teaching
behaviors, answer the following questions:

   1. How would I reach the objective using the direct
   models?
   2. How would I reach the objective using the indirect
   models?
   3. How much time should be allotted to these
   objectives? By listing the various direct and
   indirect teaching skills and models and
   estimating activity and strategy time, teachers
   should begin to list the teaching processes that
   most effectively and efficiently attain the
   intended pupil outcomes. (Remember to take into
   account all other factors present in the
   teaching/learning situation, that is, available
   materials, knowledge of the pupils' learning
   styles, games, classroom constraints, etc.) When
   a teaching model is listed as the teacher
   behavior, it will be assumed that the teacher
   can implement that model effectively in the
   sequence.

4. Materials. The purpose here is to remind the

teacher of the need to provide appropriate materials for the activities. This serves as an administrative function for pre-preparation and/or collection of materials, films, etc. It also serves as a guide to attend to the administrative details needed for such things as parental permission for field trips, etc. A well-implemented strategy will have taken all of these factors into account prior to implementation.

The last few activities of the strategy should be developed to test the attainment of the objectives. The ultimate effectiveness of any strategy is the extent to which the pupils achieved the objectives as planned. The data collected from the strategy then aid the teacher in developing further strategies and/or modifying other ongoing strategies.

After completing the planning for strategy, check it over. Does it include all of the required components? Figure 7.3 provides a checklist to see if the strategy

		Yes	No*
1.	Are outcome objectives clearly stated?	___	___
2.	Are several types of objectives included?		
	Knowledge	___	___
	Thinking	___	___
	Attitudes	___	___
	Social Skills	___	___
	Academic Skills	___	___
	Other (state) _____	___	___
3.	Are the objectives appropriate for the intended learners?	___	___
4.	Are the objectives measurable?	___	___
5.	Are the pupil behaviors in each activity consistent with intended learner outcomes?	___	___
6.	Are the teaching models and behaviors consistent with and appropriate for the pupil activity?	___	___
7.	Do the activities meet all the objectives? Note: Use the following matrix to determine which activities work with which objectives. A single activity may work for more than one objective. The results should provide data that tell whether some objectives are not being met by activities, and the degree of impact on any single objective.	___	___

Activity #___	Objectives			
(List appropriate activity #.)	#1	#2	#3	#4

(Use additional space if necessary.)

8. Which activities partially or fully measure the intended pupil outcomes? List them.
_____

*If No, review strategy in order to include the missing elements.

Fig. 7.3 Checklist for Analyzing a Teaching Strategy

is complete. Item #7 is very important in that teachers
can show the relationship between planned activities and
the overall objectives. There should be at least two
or more activities designed to directly influence each
objective.

EVALUATING THE STRATEGY
     The ultimate test of any sequence of teaching
activities is generally determined by the effects on
students. The end questions I always ask are: Did the
students attain the objectives? If so, to what degree?
This information is what parents and administrators want
to know, and it is sometimes used as a basis for teacher
evaluation.
     We all know, however, that regardless of how well
planning has been done, circumstances outside of a
teacher's control sometimes intervene in the
implementation of the learning process. Teachers must
be flexible in the implementation of the strategy as well
as able to work with unanticipated events. In order to
accommodate these variables, a strategy evaluation plan
should be developed. Teachers can use this process, in
part or in total, when implementing their strategy.
Basically, an evaluation plan asks how teachers will
evaluate each activity in the strategy. For instance,
looking at activity #1 in Figure 7.2, the evaluation of
the activity would be preserved by the recording of
student responses on butcher paper and matched with the
concepts desired by the teacher. Note that the type of
evaluation procedure can be planned prior to implementing
the strategy. Once the activity is completed, however,
the teacher must make some decisions based upon the
results. Although activity #1 on the evaluation example
does not show what happened when the activity was
implemented, let's speculate on what decisions a teacher
could make.
     First, the activity results could show that the
student responses and concepts met the teacher's
expectations and the decision would be to proceed to
activity #2; or, if the students did not fully achieve
the desired concepts, the teacher could:

1. Go on to the next activity and abandon these results.
2. Go on to the next activity, hope the students learn
   the concepts from the other activities, and then
   recheck the concepts at a later time.

Name _____

Strategy _____

Activity #	Part 1: Evaluation Planning (Type of Evaluation Procedure to be Used)	Part 2: Results of Planned Evaluation (What Did Occur)	Part 3: Decisions based upon Results
1.	Items, groups, and labels of Depression era as given by students—matched with concepts of poverty, prejudice, justice, as desired by teacher analysis of the activity and with predetermined concepts in mind.		
2-3.	Student identification of the desired concept as judged by the teacher (justice-prejudice).		
4.	Same as #1.		
5-6.	Teacher judgment of student nonverbal feedback during activities.		
7.	Videotape of activity--pupil assessment of role playing. Teacher self-assessment using role playing teacher evaluation checklist.		

Fig. 7.4 Teaching Strategy Evaluation Format: Activity Evaluation Section

3. Interject another activity that will provide the
    desired information to the students; also add another
    activity sometime later in the sequence using the
    same questions and teaching model to determine student
    growth.

    Teachers make these decisions every day. I think
many of these decisions are based upon feelings a teacher
has about a lesson rather than some type of planned
evaluative feedback that provides a logical data-based
assessment. All too often we "hope" the students learn
what we want them to, rather than doing everything we
can to be more accountable for pupil learning.
    Not every activity needs a formal evaluation process.
Note the examples for evaluation activities #2 through
#17. Teacher observation and judgment are important,
as is receiving information about the activity process
from students. Too often all we collect from students
are cognitive data (test scores, papers, etc.). Students
can help us learn to plan strategies by letting us know
what works well and what does not. By involving students
in this process, we can also better assess the learning
styles of small groups and individuals in the class.
    Finally, teachers must not neglect to evaluate how
well they are using different teaching techniques.
Activity #7 provides a clue concerning self-evaluation.
The first part of the activity evaluation concerns student
assessment of the experience. Note that the activity
is being videotaped. As the role playing model has nine
phases, and an instrument for self-evaluation is
available, this is an ideal opportunity for the teacher
to check whether he or she is using the model
effectively. If a videotape is not available, he or she
could ask a peer or superior, perhaps the principal, to
observe--but let the observer use an appropriate
observation tool, one that matches what the teacher is
trying to do. Feedback of this type is more beneficial
to teacher growth than most of the general types of
evaluations currently being used.
    The last page of the evaluation plan is an overall
summary of the effectiveness of the strategy. The data
compiled on this page let the teacher know how many pupils
attained each objective and, more importantly, allows
the teacher to analyze why (or why not) the objectives
were attained. Many events affect classroom activities,
pupils, and teachers, and I firmly believe that many of

Name _____

School _____

Grade _____

This form may be used to summarize the overall strategy and to determine reasons for attainment of objectives, based upon all activities.

Strategy Title: _____

Overall Results (Descriptive):

1. Were the objectives listed in Figure 7.2 attained? To what degree?

    a.

    b.

2. What replanning was necessary during the implementation?

3. List unanticipated events that affected the implementation.

4. What were the probable causes for outcomes?

5. What parts of the strategy will be used again? What changes will be made?

Fig. 7.5   Teaching Strategy Evaluation Summary

these are beyond a teacher's control. Assemblies, fire
drills, late films, and sirens are examples of things
that intervene in any given day, and do disrupt the
teaching-learning process.

The evaluation summary page serves as the
documentation of an accountable teacher--one who is not
afraid to explore, scientifically, what has happened in
the classroom, and to use the experience as a tool to
learn and grow professionally and personally. It lets
our students, colleagues, and superiors know that we are
accountable professionals.

A FINAL WORD

Teachers sometimes use the argument that strategy
planning and evaluation take too much time. I have heard
it said that there is too much content to cover; all the
teaching time is needed to make sure that the students
learn the content.

It seems to me that if our job as professional
teachers is to motivate students to attain the objectives
we set out, then content and time become secondary. We
choose from the content those topics that are most
important, and make sure that all of the students learn
those. I do not believe our chances of having all
students remember all the information available is
practical. So the argument becomes moot. What we can
guarantee is that students will attain the objectives
we have set out in our strategies.

Models of teaching have proven to be valuable assets
to successful teachers who wish to further improve their
teaching repertoire and learn to vary their instruction
in order to meet learner needs. The use of the models
and strategies has been proved successful in different
parts of the country with hundreds of teachers. The
strategy concept has proved to be valuable in many
aspects, the most valuable for teacher accountability.
In this era of parental demand for more effective
schooling, it is quite likely we can't do without it.

REFERENCES AND SUGGESTED READINGS
Berliner, David C., and Tikunoff, William J. "The
     California Beginning Teacher Evaluation Study:
     Overview of the Ethnographic Study." Journal of
     Teacher Education 27(1976): 24-30.

Borich, Gary D. The Appraisal of Teaching. Reading,
    Mass.: Addison-Wesley, 1977.
Eggen, Paul D.; Kauchak, Donald P.; and Harder, Robert
    J. Strategies for Teachers. Englewood Cliffs,
    N.J.: Prentice-Hall, 1979.
Flanders, Ned A. Analyzing Teaching Behavior. Reading,
    Mass.: Addison-Wesley, 1970.
Gage, N. L. The Scientific Basis of the Art of
    Teaching. New York: Teachers College Press, 1978.
Joyce, Bruce R. Selecting Learning Experiences:
    Linking Theory and Practice. Washington, D.C.:
    Association for Supervision and Curriculum
    Development, 1978.
Joyce, Bruce R, and Weil, Marsha. Models of Teaching.
    2d ed. Englewood Cliffs, N.J.: Prentice-Hall, 1980.
Joyce, Bruce R.; Brown, Clark C.; and Peck, Lucy.
    Flexibility in Teaching. New York: Longman, 1981.
McDonald, Frederick J. "Report on Phase II of the
    Beginning Teacher Evaluation Study." Journal of
    Teacher Education 27(1976): 39-42.
Rosenshine, Barak. "Recent Research on Teaching Behaviors
    and Student Attainment." Journal of Teacher
    Education 27(1976): 61-64.
Weil, Marsha, and Joyce, Bruce. Information Processing
    Models of Teaching. Englewood Cliffs, N.J.:
    Prentice-Hall, 1978.
Weil, Marsha, and Joyce, Bruce. Personal Models of
    Teaching. Englewood Cliffs, N.J.: Prentice-Hall,
    1978.
Weil, Marsha, and Joyce, Bruce. Social Models of
    Teaching. Englewood Cliffs, N.J.: Prentice-Hall,
    1978.

8

CLASSROOM MANAGEMENT

Charles Moore

Classroom management is a major topic of concern in education today. Polls show that discipline is the number one concern of parents of school-aged children. Very often the issue is the chief concern of new teachers and future teachers. In fact, discipline should be the concern of everyone involved with education. Teaching is not effective if a major portion of the class period or school day must be spent disciplining students rather than helping them to learn.

The National Society for the Study of Education (NSSE) devoted its entire 1979 yearbook to the discussion of classroom management issues. From this volume of information, several major principles emerged as being important to beginning as well as practicing teachers. Almost all education researchers have agreed that without good classroom management skills, a positive, healthy learning environment cannot exist, and without such an environment it is extemely difficult for students to progress toward some stated learning goals. The effectiveness of management schemes is related to a variety of student outcomes ranging from achievement to attitudes. If students feel they have not achieved their goals they are likely to reflect their frustration by withdrawing (saying and/or doing nothing), and/or acting out their frustrations. In either situation, the students are signaling the teacher that the classroom environment should be reevaluated.

Often, new teachers possess good skills in choosing subject matter, in teaching, and in selecting materials, but they have poor classroom management skills. Without

the ability to manage classrooms, teachers are surely
doomed to failure.

Let us look at an example. A few years ago a teacher
came to our school system to spend the entire year
learning the skills of teaching. During the preservice
interview we identified a good command of subject matter
and good interpersonal skills. As a result, this person
was hired. It was only a short time after the school
year had begun that problems began to emerge.

During the early stage of trying to analyze why
things were going wrong it became apparent that this
teacher did not have a plan for classroom management.
Violent swings from one extreme to another were
displayed. Some days the slightest noise or distraction
was met with severe consequences while on other days a
similar behavior was ignored. There was no consistency.
Needless to say, the students were as confused as the
teacher. No discussions had been held as to how to
conduct oneself in the classroom; no definitions of
accepted behavior had been made, nor had the simplest
of classroom rules been identified. In short, no ongoing
classroom management scheme existed.

This teacher was weak in management skills and he
failed in his assigned task of helping students learn.

CLASSROOM MANAGEMENT DEFINED

From a theoretical perspective, classroom management
consists of: time management, learning theory, personnel
theory, curriculum development, decision making,
instructional development, planning, and evaluation
models.

Let us examine briefly each of these eight points.

1. Managing a classroom means knowing how to use allotted
   time wisely. If fifty minutes to complete an
   assignment is allotted and it takes fifteen minutes
   to take roll, give announcements, and clean up at
   the end of the period, the remaining thirty-five
   minutes is all that is left to do a job that takes
   fifty minutes. How time segments are planned and
   organized to implement the lesson plan is important.
   Wasting student learning time usually wins no respect
   from them.
2. How do students learn? Understanding concepts of
   learning theory is a vital prerequisite for effective

classroom management planning. For instance, if an inappropriate lesson has been planned because the conceptual level was either too high or too low, then the likelihood of acted out behavior increases.

3. How to handle problem students; when and how to promote students in the classroom; and how to handle a reward system for the classroom can be learned from personnel theory. While the situations may not be exactly parallel or directly related to classroom management schemes, a great deal can be learned from personnel theory.

4. Curriculum development is another important area in classroom management. It is necessary for teachers to know how to construct a series of lessons that are in harmony with the school's curricular goals. Many school systems do not have such goals clearly defined or readily available. It is essential for a new teacher in the system, regardless of previous experience, to ascertain the working philosophies relating to curriculum. Many times, curriculum goals are the result of intensive work by teachers, administrators, parent groups, community persons, and, sometimes, students. For example, a school district may have a K-12 curriculum goal to present information that would help to eliminate prejudice. Students exposed to such lessons only in some grades and classes but not all, will likely distrust the legitimacy of the curriculum goal. This, of course, would be unfair to the students and the community groups who had helped to develop the goal.

5. Knowing when to make decisions and abiding by them helps to make classroom management easier. Many teachers fall short in the art of being consistent, yet the principle is most reassuring to students.

6. Using a variety of instructional techniques makes life in the classroom pleasanter for both students and teachers. Not all students learn in the same manner: some are visual learners and some are audio learners; some have difficulty reading and some have hearing impairment; some are highly motivated and some are not motivated at all. It may be necessary to present the same material in a variety of ways in order to reach as many students as possible. In so doing, all students are given a chance to learn. Being able to use a variety of teaching techniques

makes for an effective lesson and usually an effective lesson all but eliminates the need for classroom discipline.

7. To be an effective classroom manager, teachers must be able to plan--both for long and short term. Long-term planning in this case refers to a semester, or a quarter, or any marking period that is most convenient. Short-term planning could refer to daily or weekly lesson plans, probably both. Good planning also allows an effective manager to be flexible and willing to take advantage of spontaneous learning activities as they occur.

8. Finally, competent managers know how to evaluate current class environments. Continuous evaluation provides a means to gather and analyze feedback for improvement of the management scheme. There are many ways to evaluate; a few are: observation, opinionnaires, and consultant participation. All these offer feedback that helps in becoming a more effective teacher.

If teachers combine these eight characteristics and use them, they are headed toward proactive classroom management. Effective classroom management allows teachers to plan for events and keep them from having to constantly deal with minor infractions.

CAN THE MANAGEMENT SCHEME GO WRONG?

What happens if the management scheme is not working? What happens if a disruptive student is in the class? At what point is the teacher going to need to use discipline techniques? Discipline is not synonymous with classroom management, although the two terms tend to be confused by some. The difference is that management is proactive and discipline is reactive.

When situations arise that call for disciplinary measures, the following procedures may be helpful. First, find out precisely what happened. If more than one student is involved in the disturbing activity, it is usually best to separate them first and then ask each what happened. Separating students, besides isolating them from their peers, allows the teacher a chance to work with each student on a one-to-one basis. It eliminates peer pressures that may cause continuing disruptive behavior in the classroom.

Once the students are settled down, the next step

is to get the individual(s) to accept responsibility for what happened. If the student accepts responsibility for the inappropriate behavior, then what occurs next is much easier.

The next step is simply to explore alternative behaviors the student may have used but did not, and then outline the consequences of what happened. It is also important to outline what will happen if the student's behavior is not corrected.

To have an effective, proactive classroom management scheme, teachers need to develop a lesson plan that is incorporated into the total classroom setting. As this is developed it is wise to include the students. After all, classroom management involves an entire group.

Once the initial plan has been developed, two other important tasks are most helpful: first, provide for periodic review of the plan and allow for any revisions that may be necessary, and second, put the plan in writing.

Once the plan is in written form, whether it is on a bulletin board or in individual copy form, it becomes difficult for anyone to offer the "I didn't know" excuse. This eliminates any confusion or second guessing and insures consistency.

BEFORE IMPLEMENTING THE CLASSROOM MANAGEMENT PLAN

Before putting the management lesson plan into operation, first determine answers to the following questions:

1. How large or small is the classroom--both in physical setting and numbers of students?
2. What is wanted--an open classroom or a more traditional classroom setting?
3. How is the school climate defined?
4. How are other teachers characterized?
5. What will the other teachers accept in terms of classroom plans?
6. How much planning help will the other teachers and administrators offer?
7. Is there a counselor or an assistant principal to go to for help?

Each classroom setting will probably require some variation in the approach used. Courses may need to be approached in different ways. For example, the time of

day and whether the course is required or elective may
be important factors in developing the classroom scheme.

Whatever the circumstances, it is best to be
overprepared. It is best to plan for every contingency
ahead of time rather than trying react on the spot.

SUGGESTIONS FOR IMPLEMENTING A MANAGEMENT PLAN

Aside from communications, the following suggestions
should be implemented, but in no particular order.
Communications are a special issue because they can be
a cure-all or, if not established properly, can be the
root of many discipline problems.

To be an effective teacher, avenues for communication
must be open. Teachers must learn how to use the phone
effectively and how to write an effective letter. An
early communication to the parents may be important.
Try not to rely on the counselor or assistant principal
to make the contact with parents--it is usually more
effective if the teacher makes it since he or she knows
the magnitude of the prevailing situation. Usually, if
someone else does the communicating, they are at a loss
for answers and will need to make further contact with
the teacher, thus prolonging the communication and the
action.

Two other related practices should be followed:
first, the administrative office should be informed even
if the teacher handles a problem. This is especially
helpful if problems with a particular student continue.
Because the office has been informed, administrators know
the teacher has worked with the student and they also
have an idea of what the teacher has tried to do. Second,
keep accurate records. Records do not have to be lengthy
and formal, but they should show:

1.   Attendance
2.   Up-to-date overall grades
3.   Some form of daily participation grades
4.   An informal, anecdotal record of classroom behavior

Perhaps we can learn from William Glasser and use
a positive approach to discipline whenever possible.
To set the stage for a positive approach set the ground
rules early (as few as possible) and consistently follow
through. It is a good idea to let the students help in
establishing the classroom rules and procedures. I have

mentioned this before; when students have a stake in events, they are more apt to abide by the rules and procedures. <u>Do not be afraid to tell students what is expected of them. In most instances, they appreciate the honesty and leadership.</u>

If one teacher only is having trouble with a particular student he or she should look at the classroom and his or her own behavior to find the solution to the problem.

If most other teachers in a system are having similar problems with the same student, then. they should pool their resources and try to solve the problem together. This is called <u>crisis intervention</u>. What it involves is compiling as much data as possible about the student's behavior and then, in a conference with the parents, the teachers, the student, and the administrator, confronting the student with the findings. Sometimes this is all that is needed for a student to realize that his or her behavior was unacceptable. Once confronted, the student will often take corrective action without much interference from anyone. If that does not work, at least a vehicle as been established for prescribing remediation.

Teachers need to listen closely to both individual students and the total classroom; it is important to distinguish between the two. Each requires different skills. Being able to listen to an individual requires being able to be empathetic and not always judgmental. In the classroom, feedback should be given frequently so that both the teacher and students understand what is being communicated. Students do not like to second-guess the teacher.

Teachers can be aware of the group process that is taking place by listening to a whole classroom. But it may also be wise to be a little deaf. If a teacher reacts to everything he or she hears in the classroom he or she may be a "basket case" by the end of the day. Common sense may well be the prevailing force here.

Good classroom managers are consistent. If a teacher's standards do not permit gum chewing, then it should not be permitted. But do not change the rule the very next day or week. However, if time proves a rule is not effective, the teacher should change it and let students know.

Teachers have the responsibility to be leaders in the classroom. This means that the buck stops here and the teacher must assume responsibility for whatever

happens in education or discipline. This does not mean
that teachers are out there alone. It does mean that
teachers have to make the initial decisions that will
affect the outcome of a potential discipline situation.
Remember, it is almost always better for teachers to
handle their problems than to call in the principal.
However, teachers should not fear to call in the principal
or counselor when they have reached the end of their
ropes. Remember, we are all in this profession together.
It is a really fine line between knowing when to send
a student to the principal and keeping the matter within
the classroom.

It may be difficult at times, but it usually pays
high dividends to keep a sense of humor. Humor has
defused many serious situations. A teacher's use of humor
encourages students to like him or her as a person, an
important factor in any management situation. At the
same time, it is equally important for students to respect
the teacher. Most teachers, given the choice between
being liked or respected, prefer to be respected.
However, most often the two attributes are combined.

Handle problems or issues immediately, and know
behavior modification techniques. It is not good practice
to ignore negative behavior and hope it will go away.
Many times, students act out resentment to see how much
teachers will tolerate. Do not overreact! At times,
the teacher, by responding negatively to the student's
behavior, may actually be reinforcing the negative
behavior.

Along these same lines, teachers should not make
demands they cannot meet. They should not threaten (it
creates a challenge situation) and they should not use
extra schoolwork for punishment. If they do use
schoolwork, then the schoolwork becomes the negative
reinforcer and the student begins to associate it with
punishment. In many instances it is the student's failure
to cope with school that is causing the acting out and
if teachers add more schoolwork to this situation it is
somewhat like adding fuel to the fire.

Keep in mind it is not a good practice to punish
the whole class for the actions of a few. No matter what
the teacher says, he or she has determined the punishment
and will be held responsible by those in the class who
are innocent.

Another factor to keep in mind when organizing a
classroom management scheme is to try to begin small when

dealing with a discipline problem--do not overreact and use big guns (major consequences) right away. After the most significant consequence is used nothing is left to use when working with that particular student. Other students are going to be aware of this also and they may not react in the way the teacher wants because they have seen what the teacher does and they are not concerned with the consequences. Leave avenues open to rethink the situation--in other words, don't burn all the bridges.

It is important to keep in mind that not all students need to be treated alike nor should they be. Being fair does not mean that each student receives the same consequences for similar acts. Notice that the word punishment is not being used; it makes more sense to outline and delineate consequences than it does to mete out punishment. Teachers will find also that they will have more success in changing behavior if they use consequences for actions rather than punishment. When a student is punished, a nonproductive, adversarial climate is created.

Effective classroom management means effective teaching. Lesson plans must take into account the variety of learning styles that will be encountered. Many models and strategies for teaching are available. Use them! It is vitally important to use a variety of teaching models to satisfy varying learning styles.

CREATING AN ATMOSPHERE

A final point to mention here is the physical image the teacher and the classroom portray--a positive image.

A classroom can reflect the subject being taught and do it aesthetically so students feel satisfied about the room they are in. This can be accomplished with bulletin boards, mobiles, posters, book and magazine layouts, etc. If the classroom looks the part, the students will be helped in feeling the part. Therefore, getting the classroom ready is one of the very first things a teacher should do at the beginning of the school year and at the beginning of each new unit, to help set the tone for what happens in the classroom. A room cannot teach, but it can make teaching easier.

Successful teachers don't always have the best designed classrooms to work in, but successful teachers tend to have classrooms that portray "a lot of learning is going on here." The walls speak of things that are

happening as does the furniture. The very way in which
the furniture is arranged will suggest the kind of
activity the teacher is hoping to have. For example,
if group discussions are wanted, then certainly desks
or chairs should be placed in a circle so the students
can have eye contact with the others in the discussion
group. In contrast to this, small clusters of desks make
lecturing or demonstrating a difficult task. Flexibility
of furniture and being willing and able to adjust to the
situations helps make teaching situations happen.

A FINAL WORD
     Many teaching techniques work, but teachers should
keep in mind that they must develop a style of teaching
and management that suits them. Learn from others but
do not make the mistake of trying to copy them. If
students do not behave properly or learn all the material
in the classroom, world events probably will not be
altered--just because a child is having problems in school
does not mean that that person is doomed to eternal
failure. It is the teacher's responsibility to try to
help all students who enter the classroom. But remember,
not all teachers are reincarnations of John Dewey.
     Effective classroom managers are those people who
develop schemes that are prevention oriented. If teachers
are not prevention oriented, they will be just putting
out brush fires and not accomplishing the real goals of
education, which are to help each and every student reach
maximum personal and intellectual growth.
     In a basic sense, effective management means that
the staff is working together to solve problems. When
a staff is working together to solve problems, it has
achieved the optimum--its members are working together
and communicating, all for the goal of making our schools
better places to grow.

REFERENCES AND SUGGESTED READINGS
Blackman, Garth C., and Silberman, Adolph. Modification
     of Child Behavior. Belmont, Calif.: Wadsworth,
     1971.
Buckley, Nancy. Modifying Classroom Behavior: A Manual
     of Procedures for Classroom Teachers. Champaign,
     Ill.: Research Press, 1971.
Canter, Lee, and Canter, Marlene. Assertive Discipline.
     Los Angeles: Lee Canter and Associates, 1976.

Glasser, William. Schools without Failure. New York: Hawthorn Books, 1964.

Glasser, William. Reality Therapy. New York: Harper & Row, 1965.

Jessup, Michael H., and Kiley, Margaret A. Discipline: Positive Attitudes for Learning. Englewood Cliffs, N.J.: Prentice-Hall, 1971.

Kelley, Edgar A. "Developing a Lesson Plan for Classroom Discipline." Action in Teacher Education 1(1978).

Madsen, Charles H. Teaching Discipline: A Positive Approach for Educational Development. Rockleigh, N.J.: Allyn and Bacon, 1974.

Meacham, Merle L., and Wiesen, Allen E. Changing Classroom Behavior: A Manual for Precision Teaching. Scranton, Pa.: International Textbook, 1970.

Pickhardt, Carle E. "Fear in the Schools: How Students Make Teachers Afraid," Educational Leadership 36 (1978): 107-12.

Poteet, James A. Behavior Modification: A Practical Guide for Teachers. Minneapolis: Burgess, 1973.

Sloane, Howard Norman. Classroom Management: Remediation and Prevention. Santa Barbara, Calif.: Wiley, 1976.

"Special Issue: The Problems of Discipline and Violence in American Education," Phi Delta Kappan 59(1978).

INDEX

1514-4
5-08